the new NOW

KYLIE HENDERSON

The New Now © 2022 Kylie Henderson.

All rights reserved. No part of this book may be reproduced in any form or by any electronic or mechanical means including information storage and retrieval systems, without permission in writing from the author. The only exception is by a reviewer, who may quote short excerpts in a review.

This is a work of nonfiction. The events and conversations in this book have been set down to the best of the author's ability, although some names and details may have been changed to protect the privacy of individuals. Every effort has been made to trace or contact all copyright holders. The publishers will be pleased to make good any omissions or rectify any mistakes brought to their attention at the earliest opportunity.

Printed in Australia

Cover design by Shawline Publishing Group Pty Ltd

Images in this book are the copyright of Shawline Publishing Group Pty Ltd

Illustrations within this book are the copyright of Shawline Publishing Group Pty Ltd

First Printing: June 2022
www.shawlinepublishing.com.au

Paperback ISBN - 9781922751225

Ebook ISBN- 9781922751263

A catalogue record for this book is available from the National Library of Australia

The New Now

the new NOW

KYLIE HENDERSON

This book is dedicated to my Beautiful husband, Sean. You are my best friend, and I am ever grateful for this wild, crazy ride that we are on together. Our hardest times have turned into some of the greatest stories of breakthrough and grace all woven together into this incredible tapestry that is our life. I love you more than ever before, and I would not change a thing. This is our NEW NOW.

Contents

Acknowledgements	ix
Prologue	xi
Introduction	1
1 The Impossible is Possible	9
2 We Get to Choose	13
3 'No' is my new Best Friend	19
4 Speaking Life and Power	25
5 Identified in Him	37
6 Intimacy with Creation's Creator.	47
7 Cleaning the Atmosphere	51
8 Out of this world.	55
9 The Sound of Silence	67
10 Divine Health and Immortality	75
11 The Beginning or the End	93
12 Becoming	97
13 Finding Your Bliss	103
14 Lightworkers.	107
Final Words	111
About the Author:	121

Acknowledgements

Sam and Josh
   You have both challenged me, made me a better person and filled me with joy beyond measure. I love you so very much and I am so blessed to have you as my boys.

Acknowledgments

The New Now

Prologue

The silence is deafening, no motors cutting in and out, no voices talk, talk, talking, no music! No fans, no humming, only silence. The ringing in my ears gets louder the more I try to turn it off. The decision to close the doors of our vibrant and popular business is ever more real with every passing hour. Our new life and all the possibilities that this new future holds is becoming increasingly evident within the whispers at the dawning of each new day.

There have been ten of them; days that is, since this went down, and I cannot help wondering: what is next? My years are littered with unfinished projects and unfulfilled dreams. Even now, I sit down and stand up; I walk away, make coffee and hesitate. Have I really got what it takes to see the big dreams in my life become my reality? Just flood me, Holy Spirit, with divine inspiration, overwhelm me with the drunken bliss of the next. I want to be so consumed with your love, the Father's love, that fear's voice can no longer be heard. I know it is within the mystery of the unknown that I will truly find You and find myself.

It is in that place of rest when I stop striving, when the dust settles, and so too the hustle when I take a step back and just breathe. To be entwined within that elusive place where the cares and demands of this world take a back seat to the still small voice of wisdom and hope, that voice that whispers so sweetly, keep going, my daughter, my friend. I know within myself, somewhere in the caverns of my heart, that there is this place of fulfilment, a place of so much more. The revelation resounds before me, the bright lights flashing like a neon sign. It is found not in the busyness and distractions of building my own empire, that wondrous empire that's wildly prosperous and is helping to save the world. These answers I seek are found in a place that has been so foreign to us in our boxes; these answers lie in another land, another realm. They are found in that place of contemplation, found in that place of silence if only my ears would stop ringing.

My mind is in overdrive, processing future questions and thoughts. "What am I going to 'do' first? What's next for me?" As a doer, a woman of action, who now finds herself without the direction of the manual working tasks that I had become so accustomed to in the hospitality industry, I instead have a new sense of purposelessness. It is madness; finally, there is space, there is time. Finally, there is a window in the room, and it's open. Still, instead of excitement and drive, I am allowing a feeling of worthlessness to creep in. I even have a ridiculous dialogue going around in my head, "How are you going to explain away all those days filled with writing and drinking coffee, of reading and imagining up the realities of The New Now. How will you get by financially? Aren't you worried? I mean, you are not doing anything."

As an intrinsic thinker, it has been many years since I really let myself dream. Filing away that woman and all her fantasies, the dreams of all she had perpetually envisaged she could be. So much of what my younger self desired has long fallen away. Somehow as one grows older, a cynical cloud has descended upon everything; some call it maturity, others call it responsibility or growing up. I did, too, for a while; I adopted the responsibility of adulthood and all its seriousness. One morning an awakening of sorts ensured this road of seriousness was not the road I wanted to travel on. I woke and thought, 'I'm not buying into this grown-up lie because if growing up means leaving behind my dreams, creativity, sense of humour, desires, and life purpose, then I am just not up for that.' If the endless possibilities of my youth, those dreams held within my imagination, were only for the young me, then I want to be young, childlike and free forever. I want to live continuously engaged with my imagination and the endless possibilities held within that realm.

Like so many, I set out to begin this new decade on fire, ready to chew up the hours and be super productive, to make this a power year, a year of accelerated growth. A year filled with infinitely more than I could hope for, imagine or dare I say it, dream.

There were two of us in this, my husband and I and together, we made this tenacious decision to close our Hotel. It was one of the toughest life decisions we have ever had to make, knowing full well how much we would be disappointing the community, our families and even ourselves. We had heard a still, soft whisper; we felt it in our gut. It was part of moving forward, facing the disappointments and failures and being grateful for the good times. After trying to sell for over two years, nothing else was falling into place; how can we move into our future when we still have not closed the door to our past. For me, this decision and its timing was a head-start to 2020; we were getting in early, so to speak, with lots of preparation. It was time, time to make sure when January came around, I could hit the ground running. I had initiated a fitness program to prepare my mind and body for what was coming. I drew up a dream board and listed all those things to be achieved, all my goals for this crazy year. The great list of unaccomplished dreams and incomplete projects I had accumulated over the past thirty years. I squashed their completion times and delivery dates into the futuristic, supersonic age of 2020, then stood back gazing at them, feeling incredibly empowered and excited for the days ahead.

Soon after, as we were motoring through November, on track just six weeks shy of this wildly wonderful year beginning, I got sick. Completely smashed with a serious viral infection, a horrendous cough and challenging respiratory issues followed by a badly infected tooth that, over the New Year's holiday, needed to be removed. So, with all my planning and dreaming and striving, there I sat, on the first day of January 2020, physically and mentally drained. Instead of working out, eating clean and doing an Instagram LIVE post for all my crazy cool followers about what an incredible year it was going to be, I was barely able to do the most basic of household tasks. Overwhelmed with fevers, nausea and headaches, I was unable to speak; I couldn't exercise or even move as it was painful for my tooth and would bring on excessive coughing. It sounds like Covid 19; yes, however, the outbreak was still unannounced, and I hear you, get over it, right? It's true; I wasn't terminally ill; most likely, I wouldn't die from this crazy flu. People's houses were burning in unprecedented bushfires, we had just survived three years of catastrophic drought, still with no end in sight, but with my dream board hanging on the wall, I was sedentary in my small world filled with frustration, pain and disappointment, feeling a bit of a mess.

The irony of this whole thing is the fact that while all this was going on, I was writing a book – this book, 'The New Now', the one that encompasses Fearlessness, Freedom and dare I say it, Divine Health. It is about stepping into the fullness of who we are created to be. This is a book filled with keys to unlock freedom from our fears, a book that helps us to understand how we can journey with liberty, strength, hope and love into our incredible futures. The fact that I am not just a bit sick but that I am knocked for six sick is more than frustrating for me. It's 'doing' my head in. If you are an overcomer, and you have walked through some serious shit to get where you are, then you will understand that this is the part of this journey that I just had to press through. As we bring something of significance to completion, it would be incredibly surprising to me if there were not some hurdles and roadblocks along the way.

Strangely enough, the sweet voice I could hear in the midst of my frustration was the one that whispered REST. I had to find my Selah, my Shalom. Completing this project was now less about the doing and more about the being; it was about being still and listening. This forced downtime was about moving forward into the shadows, into the dark cloud of the presence of the Father and discovering connection with Him with oneness and with our hearts. He was leading me to the fossicking fields where I was on a discovery tour, finding the gems hidden away for such a time as this. It was taking the time to uncover these treasures and to place them in the light so others could see and know about that power that was held within every facet of their being. This was far more than just releasing a book for the sake of getting the job done. This was laying bare my shortcomings, well, a few of them anyway; we will need a few more books to tell of them all. It's being real enough to know that if we stop resting, we stop moving. If we stop learning, we stop moving. If we stop being teachable, we stop moving. If we think we have arrived, we stop moving; but if we stop moving for moving's sake, we begin to awaken, and we begin to truly come alive.

Did I really want to share with you all my sickness stories? Would that mean you will not buy my book? Contracting this viral infection almost stopped me from completing the writing of this amazing story because there is nothing like the voice of doubt to bring things to a standstill. That voice of doubt chips away resolve, 'Who are you to have answers for these people?' 'Look how sick you are.' 'You are not a doctor.' 'You are not a physician for heaven's sake', that voice seeks to remove all authority and truth. If you are reading this, celebrate, for I have pushed through, an ordinary woman overcoming myself and my own doubts and fears, knowing that I do have a testimony of healing and hope to share with you, and it can and will set people free.

Introduction

All over this incredible world, humanity is now walking into the unexpected and the unknown in a truly unprecedented way. I was to have been attending a gorgeous wedding on the Gold Coast tomorrow and another in California later in the year; both were cancelled. I am certain that this worldwide pandemic has upended countless plans and dreams and that it has placed question marks over lives, businesses and relationships alike. If all my good intentions had gone according to plan, this book would already have been released, and there would have been no mention of this worldwide pandemic within its pages. At a point in time where we find ourselves facing the unknown pathways of the future, it is now that our lives have the potential to change the face of our world and the future of the generations to come forever.

I was talking about that future, back before this whole thing began to unravel. Our bright and wonderous future filled with laughter and good times with green meadows to frolic in, a future filled with banquet tables and wine poured out without measure, with bright shining faces and the holistic wellbeing of the body, mind and soul. A future spent in Zen, that place where everything comes into alignment and truth, is where we live; Fen Shui, where there is balance and continuity, where the pictures on the walls are straight, and the cushions on the lounge are perfectly in place, where I am intrinsically woven into nature and nature into me. And now we find ourselves spinning out of control. But are we really? Spinning out of control? Or is this the very place where perspective can land and where the fulfilment of everything we ever dreamt of can begin?

In his book The Torch and the Sword, Rick Joyner says, 'You will fail in your purpose if you care what men think of your work. You must only care what the Lord thinks of it. You are here to build a movement that never stops moving. A river never stops moving; the Spirit never stops moving; if you stop, you will have departed from the way of the spirit and the way of life. You must honour the fathers and mothers to bring forth the sons and the daughters. When you become part of the New Creation, your weaknesses are transformed into strengths.'

So, where does this leave us with so many unknowns ahead? It can leave us in a position where our internal dialogue becomes 'Not Enough'. Not enough time, not enough money, over and over again. That destructive dialogue of not enough time, not enough money is not going to get us anywhere. 'No time' is a lie; we give ourselves time when we stop, we let go of everything we do out of obligation, everything we do because we have to. We simplify, if we must, the complexities of the lives that have created this 'no time' vortex of endless stress and worries and broken dreams. Given time within the lockdowns, business closure and quarantine, a little window was opened into everything that could and might be. I believe in-the-midst of everything that is happening across the earth, we have arrived at a moment 'in time', a moment of Divine Exchange.

We are returning those things we have come to realise that we do not need, and we are stepping into a place of gratitude for what we already have. It was amusing to hear a news story of a lady who, during the onset of the Coronavirus shutdowns in Australia, had panic bought over a year's supply of toilet paper. Realising what she had done and how unnecessary it was to have so much toilet paper stored up in her house, she tried to return the paper to the store. She was told there were no refunds for items like toilet paper.

Our Heavenly Father, on the other hand, is totally into the exchange. He is just waiting for us to return all that junk we know we don't need and open up to us those things that have always been there for us to lay hold of. Perhaps you have a picture like this one hanging in your life. A picture of brokenness, and He wants to exchange it for completeness. A picture of sickness, and He wants to give you health. Your picture could be a cell with bars; it's an illusion because He is the key, and He has already set you free.

Now, if you don't know anyone spiritual, then this will be a total trip. This discovery will be filled with missing pieces you never knew existed, with revelation, hope and joy as you explore the wonder and mystery that is just crying out to be a part of your life. If you find yourself struggling like me, not tapped into the river of joy, not experiencing true freedom and life, living short of the overflow of goodness that He died to give you, then let's pull out the big bunch of freedom keys and start unlocking the doors.

I had been telling myself, 'I am not enough,' am I wrong

about this? It would not be the first time that I am wrong, that is, although I do not care to admit it. I can dress up, smile and play successful. I can look like I've got it all together. After all, I'm keeping up appearances, and I would not want 'being wrong' to seep in there and mess the whole thing up. Seriously though, that mind-numbing, dream destructive dialogue of 'not enough' is erroneous; it is just a straight-up lie. That 'not enough' rubbish, along with many other lies we tell ourselves, will be dispelled as together we negate the pages of this down to earth and ridiculously real rendition of the NEW NOW.

This is a Self-Help or, more truthfully put, a 'letting go of self' help book and embracing all that is already within us. Embracing our identity as sons and daughters of Yahweh, the creator of all, and discovering our true destiny woven into our hearts' desires from before the beginning of time. As we discover who we are and what that gives us access to, we can begin to walk in the revelation that we are here to do far greater things than Jesus did; crazy, right? Creating matter out of thin air, telekinesis, bilocation, time travel, becoming invisible, working with weather systems and healing our bodies. We are together navigating the unknown ways, the ancient paths of our new world and this unity will see the restoration of so much. Do we dare to believe in the restoration of all things? Do we dare to become oneness?

I am limitless in my capacity to breathe, grow and to see. I am limitless in my capacity to build, create and to renew. I am limitless in my capacity to revolutionise the world around me with the light and sound that comes from within. I have what it takes to do this right now.

I have within me a bubbling brook of potential. Potential to give, to be, to champion and to love. To believe in, to seize, to heal and to love. Potential to open, to dream, to close and to love.

Somehow the melting pot of success pushed so many entities, so many ideas onto my ever-elusive plate, and I have emerged from beneath the flames feeling the need to be successful at them all. Success is one of those weird things; it's like, "How do we gauge it? How is it measured? Success for one is not the same as success for another. We are highly individual, we are unique, yet we are one. We tend to put our version of success onto others, and we are ever so harsh on ourselves. Our cynical culture has bred an army of critics. We take it upon ourselves to give our opinions on everything we encounter. We are a world of food critics, cleanliness critics, film critics and general people critics. Everything we experience, we see it as our right to be overly harsh and judicious if we so choose.

We are all-powerful, and we do, in essence, all get to choose. Another wonderful tangent of conversation: choices and consequences, choices and responsibility.

How did we get here? I mean, so far off track? I'm sure I was writing a book about how to get ahead in life and how to achieve your dreams, how to experience Divine Health and Immortality. I guess at some point, it may end up in a conversation about distractions, choices, destiny and, dare I say it, responsibility. Just breathe, and let's get back to the BLISS.

Let Go!!

That is where I am at. I am letting go of my preconceived ideas about the world and myself. I am allowing myself to be completely free, to be immersed in rest. Not the lying around kind of rest; I am not so good at that, but the kind of rest that does what I can within my ever-expanding capacity and trusts

God with what is currently out of my reach. I have a limitless capacity that I am only beginning to tap into. That perhaps is why there's a sense of everything being out of my control. Rest is a place of peace and wholeness; it's also a place of refreshment and joy.

"Are you weary, carrying a heavy burden? Come to me. I will refresh your life, for I am your oasis. Simply join your life with mine. Learn my ways, and you will discover that I'm gentle, humble, easy to please. You will find refreshment and rest in me." (Matthew 11:28-29 TPT).

I wonder what our world would look like if we were all awakened to the power and potential that is held within our true identities as sons and daughters of the Creator of the universe. What would it look like for us all to be awakened to our eternal destinies written before the beginning of time, found within Him Yahweh, and found within ourselves? That place whereby we have come to the ever-expanding revelation that we have been created by and held within the Creator of the universe Himself. That same creator gives us access to an expanse of untapped limitlessness as we discover that we are in Him, and He is in us. Weather patterns, droughts, floods, sickness, disease, poverty, mental health, and environmental degradation are all within our spheres of influence. All creation is essentially crying out for the sons of the Creator himself to understand who they are and begin releasing light and sound to everyone and everything within their individual and corporate realms of authority. As we discover our eternal destinies, we discover that we have a very real purpose and that it transcends space and time.

"You saw who you created me to be before I became me! Before I had ever seen the light of day, the number of days you planned for me were already recorded in your book. Every single moment you are thinking of me! How precious and wonderful to consider that you cherish me constantly in your every thought!" (Psalm 139:16-17 TPT)

What's next? How do I live like this? How can I possibly comprehend all that is in store for me? How do I take authority in all the areas and realms of my life? So often, it feels like trusting is fate or luck, giving off the impression that everything is out of my hands. Trusting is not luck or fate; trusting is letting go! Trust is not worrying and not having to be in control of everything all the time. I hear the whisper of limitlessness; I hear your sweet assurance Papa God, of more beyond. I sense a rumbling within the very core of my being; it's releasing a vibration that shakes the epicentre of the earth, crying, 'Rise Up, beautiful ones and recognise that this is your NEW NOW; you must see that nothing is ever going to be the same again.'

1 The Impossible is Possible

Have you ever wondered if the impossible were truly attainable? Healing ourselves, creating a tangible substance out of the air, or even impacting global weather patterns from our loungerooms? Is it possible to influence the phenomenon that is said to be fate or simply out of our control? The answer is YES! We are far more powerful than we could ever have imagined or believed. This revelation is not just for a select few; it is for all those who choose to take hold of it, stepping into the wonder of all their future holds. We all can impact the possible with the impossible, you and me, the everyday people, because this is THE NEW NOW.

I have watched my children navigate an interesting era filled with rapid technology growth and a progressively inept education system struggling to cope with the huge range of seemingly highly dysfunctional children being funnelled through its doors. Education, its law, is a right. However, it is also one of the very few options for parents in our society filled with so much busyness, so many commitments, and so little time. We really don't have the resources to customise our lives to the changes within our culture and world to accommodate this new generation of incredible people rapidly infiltrating our culture and world. We just don't have the time to understand, or do we? Just because we know something does not mean it has become a practical reality in our lives. Knowledge is only a part of change, for we as a people must be activated in that knowledge for it to become our truth.

As we make decisions combining information, revelation and activation, then we will begin to see a generation of global impactors and overcomers walk this earth. People who know who they are and are no longer afraid. It is when we move from purely knowing and believing something to being activated and living within the reality of that knowledge that we will begin to be the change. Our hearts, that is where the revolution begins; it's where we find our identity, our destiny and our worth. The exciting consequences of this maturation will be a limitless transformation of self, society, culture and reign.

I had a moment the other day that spoke so loudly to me personally. If I am only doing what I'm meant to be doing, then I can do everything; however, if something in my life is not meant to be there, I will feel overwhelmed and unable to do any of the things on my plate very well. Having spent a large portion of life with big visions and big dreams, somehow, my walk has been somewhat smaller than those dreams, smaller than what I have imagined. It has certainly been an interesting and adventurous ride; it's just been a little different from what I first saw. Added to this has been my inability to say 'no' to things I should not be involved with, good or otherwise. This tendency to be a 'yes' person has, in the past, seen me become stressed and left me with no time for the people that matter most. Taking on too much also left me overwhelmed by the small things. There is that debilitating voice inside my head again, whispering, 'you're just a dreamer.'

Come on, we were born to live a limitless life, a life filled with endless possibilities. We were designed to live on top of our world, not underneath, and to govern within our own spheres of influence in a way that sees victory and freedom in our lives and the lives of all those around us. We were created for more.

'A Wonderful Adventure' is one way to describe the process of discovering the truths I will share with you in the pages to come; another way to describe this journey is arduous, problematic and cruel, for nothing is ever quite what it seems on the outside. The unseen is ever more real than the seen, and that goes for our natural lives as much as our supernatural lives. You do not have to see it to believe it, for that, my friends, is the greatest disservice of limitation we bestow upon ourselves as we set out to attain the impossible. To first see something in the tangible realm before we believe it is possible negates the latter straight away. Many a person has said these words, "If I see it, then I'll believe it", and even when a miracle presents itself, they have buried that seeable truth under a pile of doubt and unbelief.

Rise up and seize all that is before you, push forward into the day, make the tough decisions, lose the baggage, and find your bliss. You will discover that right here, in the midst of a world on its knees, is a tribe of lovers who truly believe that the Impossible is Possible. Welcome to The New Now.

KYLIE HENDERSON

Revelation – We were born to live a limitless life, a life filled with endless possibilities.

Activation – I cannot see air, but I am breathing.
Take a deep breath, breathing in this invisible wonder we call air.
Exhale; as you exhale, breathe out your need to see things before you believe they are real. Simply sit, lie down or stand with your eyes closed and do this for a few minutes.
Then say - I am filled with the wonder of breath, I don't see it, but I believe it is real.

2 We Get to Choose

Where does this NEW Now begin? It begins with a decision to move forward, full stop. My husband and I have been married for twenty-eight years, and during this time have moved twenty-six times. So, we have been living this 'moving forward' thing in an ultra-practical way. Now I'm not advocating a geographical move every time you 'move forward'; it just so happens that in our case, it has often involved moving to a new house, a new city, state and for some, like our son, moving to another country in another part of the world. One of the common factors in most of our 'moving forward' moves is the lack of details about how everything is going to work out. I really get that whole story of Abraham leaving his father and mother and going somewhere though he did not know where; he just knew he had to go. Abraham is one of the guys in the Christian Bible that we call a 'Father of Faith'. That is a person whose life story displayed a great amount of Faith-based decisions or decisions that meant moving forward without all the details. It's tapping into something that is beyond what we know and understand. Faith enables us to believe that there is more for us, more for our family, and in Abraham's case, more for the future generations that would come after him. Faith is the substance of things hoped for and the evidence of things not yet seen. It's the belief that there really is more good for our world beyond what we can currently see.

So, what does that look like in a practical sense? Most recently, it looked like closing the doors to our business, our Pub and turning the building into a home. It has looked like changing careers and stepping into the great unknown. For me, that has meant time to do what I have always dreamt of. YES!! Writing this book, composing music, creating beautiful works of art, touring the nation, encouraging others in their personal relationship with our incredible Creator and sharing how He has helped me discover the power that is within me to change my world.

For my husband, it has meant starting a completely new career in a field he has never worked in before, challenging himself and embracing our rapidly changing landscape and the myriad of wonderful technologies now available right at our fingertips. It has been accepted that we are not bound by geography, that we are not bound by time. It has meant navigating the great unknown filled with impossible situations and seeing them become our possible status quo. It means seeing everything as achievable and allowing this to become our new normal way of operating, our New Now. Moving forward is hard; however, it is in that place of challenge that our dream is no longer just a dream; it truly begins to become our reality.

Now you may imagine that we closed a thriving business that had lined our pockets for the next venture in our lives. You may be thinking, 'they are so lucky to be able to do that, but my situation wouldn't allow for that,' perhaps the voice in your head is saying, "I could never do that". Maybe your perception is you just don't have enough time, enough money, enough guts?? Well, my voice was the same, AND our situation was not positioning us to make this decision of closure from an enviable place of victory and abundant wealth. We were surviving! If anything, we were slowly going backwards, not forwards. Everything we had hoped our business would eventually become and eventually pay for seemed further away than ever. All those hopes and all those dreams had all but disappeared. Now there is an element of perspective here, too, but I will talk about that later.

The point I am highlighting is our 'Moving Forward' moment was made from a place of not really knowing how it was all going to work out. It was a decision forged in the rocky place, the valley of doubt and unbelief. It was a deep knowing that if we did not, we would be far worse off than if we did. It was that nudge, that persistent, still soft voice that kept on reassuring us that He, our Creator, could be trusted to outwork through us immeasurably more than our greatest request, our most unbelievable dream and exceed our wildest imagination with what was in store. How could this be possible? How could we make it work? How could we fit it all in? Because His miraculous power constantly energizes me.[1]

There is so much mystery to living life in this way; it is no wonder that so many of us crave adventure. It's like we have been preset to live without all the answers. Yet, over the years, we have been taught that we are limited by our humanness and that we should know everything about something before we attempt to give it a real go, especially if we want any hope of success. Our thirst to acquire knowledge seems widely unquenchable. How many people do you know that do not even practice in their field of certification? The flip side is how many unqualified people in our parents' generation have gone on to defy all odds and achieve greatness in their chosen fields without a Bachelor of Business or, for that matter, without any kind of degree at all.

    I, in no way, want to take away from the educational pursuits of my peers. It is my preference, if I were in need of surgery, to be operated on by a highly educated and experienced doctor as opposed to one who had simply wanted to be a doctor and just started practising. My point here is that it is extremely hard, if not impossible, for us to acquire all the knowledge for where we are going in the NEW NOW. There are limited maps, and it would seem the ones that we do have simply point to The Father to Papa, to God to Jehovah. How do I get there? Through the Son, through Yeshua. Oh, that is just great, that is, so now I must believe that God is The Father, and He has a Son, and His Son is the Way that I get to Him, the Father. Now to further complicate things, there is also a Spirit, a Holy Spirit that is my Helper and my friend; there are also seven spirits before the throne, yes, I said throne, and then to top it all off, there are millions of Angels, many of which are assigned to you and me personally. There is a Cloud of Witnesses or, to put it in more relatable terms, a group of people who lived in bodies but have now passed away and continue to live on without their bodies and are witnessing what continues to happen on earth. It is possible at times to interact with them when they choose to interact with us, but we can't always see them. Yes, that is why this whole thing is best summed up as 'A Mystery'.

    The joy of this whole scenario is that He is found in the mystery and that I, with my feelings of inadequacy and incompleteness, become complete in the mystery, which is Him. So, I am in Him, and He is in me. I am in Him, and He is in me. I am in Him, and

He is in Me. Just say that a few times, and you will begin to understand what I am talking about when I say 'The Bliss'.

So, you see, you are powerful, you are powerful to choose. That is what makes this such an incredible journey; that choice, it means the ball is in our court. We always have everything we need to move forward, even when it feels like we don't. And it never feels like we have all we need because the missing part in the equation is Him; He is the Mysterious piece, the unknown quantity. He is the unexplainable, the immeasurable. He is the part that means risking it all, that means not knowing and still moving forward. He is that piece that means not having all the answers but one. How? Because I am in a relationship with the one who does. With the Great and Wonderful Mysterious One, with the great I AM.

Revelation – I am in Him, and He is in Me.

Activation – Find a quiet place.
Just breathe in and out
As you breathe, slowly say, "I am in Him, and He is in me."
"I am in Him, and He is in me."
Repeat this until you begin to smile; trust me, it will happen.
Let this love float over you and penetrate your whole being, resting within your heart.
Just breathe in the revelation of Him and His presence and exhale His love.

---

[1] (Footnote - reference Ep 3:20 TPT).

3 'No' is my new Best Friend

You will find as you begin to move in the right direction that you will get some open doors. Open doors are opportunities that come your way, and you can decide if you will walk through them or not. You will also get opposition that is primarily attempting to bleed you of time. You will have lots of opportunities and, to some, you will say YES, yet to many of these, you will need to say "NO". That's right, you will have to say NO. It is strange that good is often the enemy of best. There are so many good things that we can be a part of, good causes to support, good people to hang with, good jobs to take, good ideas to jump on board with, good churches to go to, good educational pursuits to attain. Getting involved with every good thing that comes along is the very worst thing a visionary can do. You see, for many of us, we see potential and solutions in everything; it is a blessing, a wonderful quality given to us by our Heavenly Father; seeing potential, seeing restoration, seeing wholeness in one another is who we are intended to be. But being intricately involved in everyone and everything's process is called 'seeing my time disappear and my dreams get further away.'

Believe it or not, it is not my job to be involved in everything. Recognising a good opportunity does not necessarily mean that it's your God opportunity. With that in mind, He did say that He will never leave me nor forsake me[2], which basically means it doesn't matter what road I take, how many detours, how many times I get bogged, distracted or lost; yes, it's possible to lose yourself in a good thing. But do not worry, for He is on all the roads on the entire journey with me, and ultimately, I will be ok.

Revelation – He is on all the roads.

Activation – Say 'No' to something this week that you know you need to say no to but have been putting it off because you don't want to disappoint anyone.
You may feel a sense of obligation or like you are letting someone down, but once you make the decision, you will feel a sense of empowerment, freedom and peace.
Embrace the freedom, and enjoy the peace.

If I am to rule and reign in my life, I must recognize what I am to be involved with and what I am not. I have struggled with this big time; however, over the past ten years, saying 'No' to those things that were taking up all my time has meant I now have more time for the new. This has meant, for me, an ever-increasing involvement in the unseen realm. It has been a great learning curve for someone who is relatively comfortable around people and has always seen themselves in the limelight. This undercover position, this role in the unseen realms, is now a place I long for more than anywhere else, as I now know and understand the power that is given and executed here. I have also come to understand my role and function in life as I further understand the greatness of all we are called to participate in here on earth and what this means for all of creation. We are human rights activists, we are wilderness warriors, we are animal lovers and spiritual guides. We interact with the trees, the rocks, and the water, and when we speak, our words change the atmosphere. By saying 'No,' we say yes to being over time, not under it, we say yes to the impossible, yes to the unimaginable, we say yes to breakthroughs, yes to dreams, we say yes to a limitless capacity to outwork what was written for our lives before the beginning of time. We say 'Yes' to our destinies, and we say yes to Love.

Yes, to Love? Absolutely. If there is one thing that goes out the window first when I say yes to too many things, it is my love for people. When I'm overworked and under-rested, and my patience tank is on empty, I just can't stand them. Perhaps I should not speak in this way; I am a Christian, for heaven's sake, should I admit that there are times in my life when 'I just don't like people'? I guess my confession is an illustration ensuring my inability to powerfully run on empty. Strangely, as much as it may seem, this situation reveals that it's not the people I don't like as much as it is myself. It is the way everything is unfolding; it's being somewhere I don't want to be and doing something I didn't necessarily want to do. It's feeling obligated and obliged; it's being overcommitted. It's micromanaging; it is doing too much, juggling everything whilst becoming overwhelmed and stressed. Often, I have been so mad at God, ranting, "Where are you?" "Why are you not helping me here?" "Why am I so stressed, so overworked, is life really meant to be like this?"

"These people don't care; they can't even see me and what I'm trying to achieve here!" This is a thankless and pressure-filled life, to which He just quietly replies, "Well, I didn't ask you to do that now, did I?"

> **Revelation** – Doing something *for* God is not the same as doing something *with* Him.
>
> **Activation** – Write down the things you think you have to do and eliminate those things that are not bearing good fruit in your life, those things that don't bring you joy.

My new best friend, 'No', is helping me to LOVE. And to not just simply love for love's sake but to completely be Love. Here is the mysterious part again, and you may have heard it before, God IS Love. The best part about that is, He is in Me, and I am in Him. If He is in me and I am in Him, then I have love in me by being in Him. This is a big spiritual health check for all you lovely church-going religious people out there, 'they will be known by their love.'[3] Not by their capacity to judge others, or their good manners, nor by their ability to recite bible verses or their verbal public opposition to all those things that are contrary to their beliefs. It is my friends, that they will be known simply by their ability to Love.

Love is the single most powerful action on earth. It defies itself in its general un-deservedness. We challenge one another as we become the very thing that most do not believe they are nor deserve. Our culture so blatantly confuses love and sex. It muddies the waters of freedom by advocating the right to say Yes as the best decision. I believe the power is in the ability and the decision to say NO. Just because we can, does not mean we should. A freedom that is aligned with choice, independence and free will is also aligned with sovereignty, truth and love. Do we choose the independent, self-determined freedom of 'Yes', or do we choose the uninhibited, liberators' choice of 'No'?

I am sure you can appreciate the context of this Yes/No debate. The point in my illustration is to embrace the freedoms found in allowing yourself to no longer make decisions from a place of obligation but rather from a place of freedom and love. I do not make the decision because I already love, I make it because I want to love, and I want to live from that place where I can love and do love effortlessly. This love comes from the endless supply I am now tapped into, an endless river, an ocean, a sea. Imagine an endless bountiful supply of love.

When I first began learning about this "being Love" thing some twenty years ago, I found myself in the supermarket standing at the checkout in a line behind two others. I began talking with the man in front of me as the person in front of him was being served. I asked how he was going, and he began to tell me a story of 'not enough'. He was explaining how everything was so expensive and he would just like some fish. Still, he had to buy these basic groceries, after which he wouldn't have enough money left to buy fish. He seemed angry at the world and unhappy with his lot in life. As the cashier began to put this man's groceries through the checkout, I just had this welling up inside me. I wanted to buy his groceries for him, and as he was facing me telling his story, I was able to lean forward and give the cashier the money for his goods. He was completely taken aback and started saying, "What are you doing? I don't understand?" I motioned to him that he should take the money he would have used to buy these groceries, and he should go and buy some fish with it. He wandered off all flustered and a little overwhelmed. So, I picked up my groceries and walked out to the carpark, where I began to load them into the boot of my car. From behind me, I could hear a guy yelling, "Hey, hey" I turned around to see the man I had been speaking to in the supermarket running across the carpark, carrying a big bunch of flowers. He ran over to me, bouquet in hand and arms stretched wide in my direction as he handed me the posy. It's probably a little over the top, but I got really cross with him, almost yelling, "What are you doing? you were supposed to buy some fish with that." He responded with sincere gratitude by saying that he had almost given up believing that there was anyone good left in the world and that my gesture that morning of buying his groceries had ignited a little flame of hope in his life again, that he no longer cared about the fish but only wanted to buy me flowers to say thank you.

We must not underestimate that loving people in very simple, kind and very different ways can one by one remove those hardened walls of humanity that say the world is lost and broken and heartless. We can be that expression in our everyday lives that is kindness and empathy and LOVE.

> **Revelation** – Love is the single most powerful action on earth.

> **Activation** – Be love in action this week; just one small thing can transform a person's day.

---

[2] (Footnote – Heb 13:5)
[3] (Footnote – John 13;35)

4 Speaking Life and Power

Our wonderful world is filled with ever-increasing rights and liberties, even if, for a time, we were in lockdown. This is exciting; however, with this has come an epidemic online and within social media, which gives us a platform to comment with complete disregard for the very real human that may be on the other side. The media often feel it is their right and even their duty to expose lies and reveal the truth, often getting the two entwined and confused. This freedom to speak is a right birthed, a personal right we all hold, to say whatever we please to whomever we want whenever we see fit to say it. I have even seen this done by well-meaning Christians under the guise of 'The truth in Love'. Bull shit! Shocked? Seriously, guys, we must stop that stuff. We need to hold ourselves accountable for the things that come out of our mouths, spoken, texted, typed or otherwise. We must understand that our words are containers of power. The power to build up or destroy, the power to discourage or encourage, to fill full of fear or to become an expression of love.

It certainly has been a learning curve for me, learning to shut up, that is. Learning that even if I have something to say, I do not always have to say it. Learning that not everyone wants my opinion, not everyone needs my opinion, as much as I might want to give it. Often it comes down to the age-old saying, "if you can't say something nice, then don't say anything at all". Learning that it is powerful to listen to people. An article by Pete Mosley on quietrev.com titled 'The power of listening: An Excerpt from "The Art of Shouting Quietly" states, "one thing quiet people tend to be good at is listening". In the seminal *How to Win Friends and Influence People*, Dale Carnegie espoused listening skills, coupled with great and genuine questions, as the way to get along in life. We love the sensation of being listened to, and the more comprehensively we are listened to, the more we respond. It is powerful stuff. We fall in love with people who listen to us; we vote for people who listen to us; we buy the products and services of people who listen to us. The ability to listen is one of the most profound influencing skills available to us.

In my twenties, I had an answer to all the world's problems, which I was quite vocal about. I had an answer for Rachel up the road's work problems. Dan's relationship problems, with my wealth of experience, I knew what he should be doing. It never occurred to me why all the older and wiser people would simply sit, smile and not even respond as I let my mouth run wild. I just presumed they were out of touch, and it was up to the younger generation to show them how it should be done. I could tell you how to cook bolognese and what colour Veronica should have painted her fence. More often than not, I was simply running people down, deflecting attention from my shortcomings whilst bringing attention to the shortcomings of everyone and anyone else. This constant talking all too often turned into gossip. Did you hear about… Can you believe the way… Oh my goodness, did she really wear that to a wedding? You are laughing, shaking your head; no, you are judging me. Well, if you are, it is probably a fair call. I needed a shakedown.

I was a tough case, a right know-it-all, a self-righteous so-and-so that loved Jesus and wanted to save the world, on my terms, of course, because seriously, nobody else had any good ideas. I also loved a good party, and I wanted to be wealthy. Sadly for a time took both into my own hands as I navigated my way forward with Jesus well and truly in the back seat of my life. The more I tried to make it on my own merits, in my own strength, the more frustrated I got and the more vocal I became about everything. I was slowly transforming from a positive world changer to a negative dream destroyer. With twenty-five looming, I felt like my dreams had slipped away, and I sure as hell did not want anyone telling me about their or anyone else's success. I was a negative, self-absorbed right royal pain in the butt. But my Heavenly Father, my Papa, my God, He was loving me, and for all the distance I perceived was between us, I was the one running away.

I needed to change everything. My attitude, the way I spoke to my husband, the way I spoke about my dreams, my aspirations, our future and my life. I had been listening to Joyce Meyer, an American bible teacher with serious attitude. If there was one thing I understood at the time, it was the place I needed to start. I had to get rid of the garbage coming out of my mouth; I had to understand that the source of life and power was in my words. I needed to start taming my tongue. I began this incredible journey of discovering the power held within the words that I speak, all of them, they all count. Words can do anything, everything. The Creator of this universe created all things with the power of words and breath.

> Anywhere and everywhere, you can find his faithful, unfailing love!
> All he had to do was speak by his Spirit-wind command,
> and God created the heavenlies.
> Filled with galaxies and stars,
> the vast cosmos he wonderfully made.
> His voice scooped out the seas.
> The ocean depths he poured into vast reservoirs.
> Now, with breathtaking wonder,
> let everyone worship Yahweh, this awe-inspiring Creator.
> Words he breathed and worlds were birthed.
> "Let there be," and there it was—
> Springing forth the moment he spoke.
> No sooner said than done!
>
> **(Psalm 33:6-9 TPT).**

It has been a process, this learning how to speak. The ups and downs, mountains and valleys, good days and challenging days, but now, over twenty years later, things have certainly changed. My life now stands on two decades of positive affirmations of speaking those things that are not as though they are. I stand on the words He says about me, on those words that have flowed through me as I developed a deeper and deeper relationship with Him. I have learned to speak the words of the Spirit over my loved ones and over myself.

His love for us and His desire to be in a relationship with us, to be intimate with us, is overwhelming. His passion for us is uninhibited and wild, casting out our fear and replacing it is to see the person they are truly becoming. When I propose that we 'declare over them' who they are, I am not speaking of the person that you see before you, the one with faults and frustrations and issues and bad habits. I am talking about the gold that lies within that person, the buried treasure that is just waiting to be recognised, discovered and drawn out. Each of us has deep within us a seed of destiny; it's a place that was birthed when we were first conceived. It's our map, blueprint, and purpose for being on the planet, and we want desperately to know what it is and begin walking it out. As we discover our identity in Yeshua, then we can be instrumental in speaking release for others into their destinies as well. This is the place and the relationship that furthermore helps us to discover our own path; it's a powerful place where a world of possibility opens up as we see ourselves and others as we were all meant to be.

This journey of discovering our multi-faceted and multi-dimensional lives is also the one that truly lets us discover our connection with each other, the déjà vu piece of ourselves, the piece that says, "We've met before" or "You were in a dream I had last night". It is part of that wonderful mystery, the one where we are in Him, and He is in us, and we are all in creation. As we are all connected in the spirit, it is possible for us to see these things in one another, for we do have a connection that is beyond what we can see with our natural eyes. We are united in this mystical oneness.

For all the good positive affirmations we may be able to put out there, it is truly a heart transformation that we desire. The ultimate place we want to end up in is the arms of the Father, the Divine, in the very epicentre of Him and His love. Everything we speak of, written here on the pages of this book, is to lead you ultimately into intimacy with Him. It is a pathway to understanding His affections for you, a journey that unfolds the realms of possibility, that presses open the windows of bliss and happiness found beyond the complexities and mess of our daily lives.

Revelation – My words are containers of power.

Activation – The next time you are with a group of people, endeavour to really hear what each person is saying.
As you listen, be guided by Wisdom, engaging with her as you press in to bring words of encouragement and love.
Ask the Holy Spirit, your helper, your counsellor and guide to prompt you in conversation. Ask Him to give you the words to speak.

I have listed below some positive and affirmative verses from the Bible that you can speak over your loved ones and yourself.

My faith does not rest in the wisdom of men but in the power of God – 1 Corinthians 2:5

You are my hiding place from every storm of life; you even keep me from getting into trouble! You surround me with songs of victory. – Psalm 32:7 TLB

I will be strong, vigorous, and very courageous. I will not be afraid, neither will I be dismayed, for the Lord with His perfect passionate love. A heart on fire revealed in this beautiful Passion Translation taken from The Song of Songs.

Song of Songs 2:10-15 TPT

Arise, my dearest. Hurry, my darling.
Come away with me!
I have come as you have asked
to draw you to my heart and lead you out.
For now is the time, my beautiful one.
The season has changed,
the bondage of your barren winter has ended,
and the season of hiding is over and gone.
The rains have soaked the earth
and left it bright with blossoming flowers.
The season for singing and pruning the vines has arrived.
I hear the cooing of doves in our land,
filling the air with songs to awaken you
and guide you forth.
Can you not discern this new day of destiny
breaking forth around you?
The early signs of my purposes and plans
are bursting forth.
The budding vines of new life
are now blooming everywhere.
The fragrance of their flowers whispers,
"There is change in the air."
Arise, my love, my beautiful companion,
and run with me to the higher place.
For now is the time to arise and come away with me.
For you are my dove, hidden in the split-open rock.
It was I who took you and hid you up high

in the secret stairway of the sky.
Let me see your radiant face and hear your sweet voice.
How beautiful your eyes of worship
and lovely your voice in prayer.
You must catch the troubling foxes,
those sly little foxes that hinder our relationship.
For they raid our budding vineyard of love
to ruin what I've planted within you.
Will you catch them and remove them for me?
We will do it together.

Looking back over these years and understanding how powerful it is to see the person He sees and acknowledge this by speaking these affirmations over my life is a true testimony of the transformational power held within our words. Time as I now understand it has been good to the process, even though if you had told me I wouldn't finish my book until I was in my forties, I'd have told you that you were mad. I am now reaping good things; yes, there's good fruit on the trees, and it tastes delicious. In other words, my relationships are stronger; Jesus is no longer in the back seat. I have learned that it is possible to be in a room and not have to command the attention of everyone by dominating every conversation. There are still mountains to climb and valleys to traverse, but I have come out the other side of this battle with my mind and my mouth.

I've learned that two timely sentences spoken softly and filled with love have more impact than the constant drone of someone that won't stop talking, somebody that thinks they have all the answers to all the questions while never listening to what anyone else has to say. I recall spending whole conversations while others were sharing their stories, thinking

God is with me wherever I go. He never rejects me but has promised to be with me always. – Joshua 1:9

And this small and temporary trouble I suffer will bring me a tremendous and eternal glory, much greater than the trouble. For I fix my attention not on things that are seen but on things that are unseen. What can be seen lasts only for a time, but what cannot be seen lasts forever. – 2 Corinthians 1:3-4

By Your Favor, O Lord, you have established me as a strong mountain – Psalm 5:12

5 Identified in Him

It's ok to be one with ourselves, to be one with nature and one another. However, if we remove from this our oneness with the Divine, with the Creator, with YHVH (Our Papa and our God) through Yeshua (Jesus), then we will still have a big gaping hole that leads us to find our identity in something or someone else.

Most of us find it easiest to align our identity with our career. People ask what we do, and that begins to frame up around us our identity. Identity can be career-based, where you might say, 'I am a doctor,' a real estate agent or a farmer. It could be a family-based identity, like 'I'm a mum', or the son of…. Perhaps your identity may be religion-based like you are a priest or a pastor. These days in our populous social media crazed society, the answer may well be that you're an influencer or an entrepreneur. But is this really us? Is that all we have amounted to, being identified as a profession?

Coupled with this successful career image is the look and lifestyle of being free. I believe this longing to be identified as free, even just with a humblebrag, to be the foundation for the huge rise of the influencer. It is a place that we long to be seen, a way of living that screams of success, of freedom and opportunity. I am being paid for being me and for doing what I love; I am travelling and eating out while venturing to long-lost wild places with picturesque horizons pressed with the perfect filters for Instagram. We long to be associated with that freedom and not be a slave to the system, banks, and restrictions put on us by the obligations and commitments within our culture and society. We long to be adventurous, to explore; we also want an eco-friendly, beautiful home and an idealistic lifestyle to come back to when all the adventuring is done. We want these things now, not in ten years, and it would be nice if we did not have to pay too much to get them, it would be nice if they too were free. Hassle-free, worry-free, debt-free and judgment-free.

My sense in all this (completely unresearched and with no surveys or official analysis and reports to back it up, it's just a feeling) is that there are a lot of influencers out there living lives that are not living up to the image or persona that they are putting out there for the world to see. Being identified as unique, free and successful are tickets to the possibilities held within the possible. While we hang onto those things that are within our reach, those things that are possible, feeling with all our inadequacies they are realistically unattainable, we will never fully embrace the mystery of the One whom we are designed to be identified in and to walk with.

Several years ago, my husband Sean, our two boys, and I spent a year living in Alice Springs in the heartland of Outback Australia. I had been regularly riding my bicycle, often traversing the streets releasing, amongst other things, declarations of freedom and love over the heartland city. One morning as I awoke, I distinctly heard instruction that prompted me to ride my bicycle into town. I had some grocery shopping to do and fifty dollars to spend doing it. So, I took some shopping bags, planning that while I was on this Holy Spirit Mission, I would pick up the necessities on the way home.

As I rode along the sandy riverbed beside the ever-thirsty Todd River, I wondered what might lay ahead, what would happen as this day unfolded, who would I encounter on my journey and what was in store as I accepted this mysterious mission. With no further insights as to where I should go next, I thought I would pick up the mail from our Post Office Box.

As I pulled up at the Post Office and dismounted my bike, I thought, 'perhaps I've got a cheque in the mail' that would be nice. Laughing, I thought, it's funny how the mind works, always thinking of itself. That was not to be, however, for when I opened the post office box, it was 'completely empty'. I thought, 'that's strange', and wondered, 'why am I here?' As I continued to stand there in front of all those post office boxes, I did feel like I was where I needed to be. So, I waited right where I was for a moment before I felt an urge to turn around. The Holy Spirit spoke to me. "See that guy over there," I surveyed the surrounding area and spotted a young Aboriginal man sitting on a bench not far from where I was standing. I answered, 'YES'. Holy Spirit went on, "He feels like your Post Office Box" ..... EMPTY.

Feelings of empathy flooded my being, and I wondered what The Lord had in store next. He told me to go over to the young man and tell him how the Father, how God sees Him. My automatic response was... "uhm, more information, please", to which He replied, "I'll tell you when you get there". He then added that once I had told him how the Father, Yahweh felt about him, that I was to give him the fifty dollars that I had brought with me to buy that week's groceries. I'll admit, I argued just a little, "but that's for the groceries", before quickly resigning myself to the fact that there was no point in arguing with the Creator of All Things; I should just shut up, walk over to this guy and see what happens.

I have said it before, it's no wonder we crave adventure, and this secret-mission style adventuring is the craziest of all. This story may not be super risky or dangerous; I'm not in China distributing bibles or in the Middle East praying for someone to be healed. I am, however, feeling a little ill-equipped to be what this guy needs right now and could, at this point, just walk away thinking that nothing I could say or do would make the slightest bit of difference to his life or to this emptiness that's now been highlighted to me. It was crowded that day at the post office, and really, did I want to make a scene?

I was here, and I'd said yes to this crazy mission, so without further postponement, I headed in the direction of this young man sitting on the bench. Walking up with my hand out to shake his, I introduced myself, explaining that I had been sent by God with a message - yes, trippy, hey? I told him that his Heavenly Father wanted me to pass on just how He saw this young guy, His son. Sounds a little out there; well, the guy was spinning out, he was speechless, so I continued. As I opened my mouth to begin, I was overwhelmed by what I can only describe as a river of love, a stream of pure bliss flowing right from the Father's heart through me and onto this guy. The words coming out of my mouth were beautiful; they were establishing him as a Son of the Creator of the Universe, a lover of people and a leader in his community. His identity was not one of loss and brokenness, abandonment and abuse; it was one of fullness and completeness; he was part of a royal priesthood. He was a king and a son. As I began to finish speaking and this river ceased to flow, we both found ourselves in tears right there beside the Post Office in downtown Alice Springs, overwhelmed by this love and generosity, undone by the goodness of a wild and mysterious God.

As I stood up to leave, still shaking from the intensity of the encounter, I opened my hand and in it was the fifty dollars. I placed it in this young man's hand and told him that the Holy Spirit had furthermore told me that I was to give this fifty dollars to him as a seal. Well, you can imagine it was just the tipping point; once again, we were both undone. I walked away, leaving that young man, who was a total stranger to me, yet a man who had always been known as an ever-loved son of Almighty God, leaving him there enlightened, connected and no longer feeling empty but now feeling very much full and very much loved.

This is the joy; it is the wonder and the mystery of being one with Him, our creator. It is this enigmatic and unexplainable connection we have with one another. As we tap into Holy Spirit and discover Him as a person, we can then discover all that opens to us in the spirit realm. When we engage with this wondrous and powerful spirit, we can be counselled in our ways and strengthened in His joy; we can attune our ear to His voice and leading. We can see others as they truly are and be a prophetic voice for someone else, speaking over them who they are in Him. That is the Truth in Love. That is being completely blissed out in the river, being filled and overflowing with the wine of His love and then opening our mouths to allow the overflow of His goodness to pour over everyone and everything that surrounds us and all who are on our horizon and in our wake.

He completes us; identifying ourselves in Him allows us to be truly ourselves. Our authentic selves, it's our truth, that place that makes sense and yet makes no sense at all; it's that place where we are filled with peace, where we can see the world whole and us as a part of it. In that place where we understand that it does not matter what we do or do not do, it's not like we have to clean ourselves up or get our lives together first. He wants us to realise that we are seen, known and loved by the Creator of All Things; we are loved completely as we are right now, in the mess. He longs for us to discover that we are intrinsically woven into this beautiful tapestry we call life. Each one of us is so unique, each one is valuable, and each one of us is overwhelmingly loved. Unity with the Divine, the cry of His heart, unity with one another, the bliss of His love. Oneness.

I was travelling through the Central West, a regional area within Australia, making my way north along the Newell Highway. Having been out of town for a few days, I was keen to get home. I had been away working, and with just over an hour and a half still left to drive, I passed through the country Mecca of Narrabri. As I motored through the centre of town, I felt that familiar nudge. "Turn here." I was not in the mood for diversions, it had been a long day, and I just wanted to get home. At the same time, I was curious, so I put my indicator on and turned up the main street. As I cruised along in my blue Ford laser hatchback with its completely smashed passenger side door due to a recent collision with a large kangaroo who was trying to hitch a free ride, I noticed a couple of young people standing on the side of the road. One of these people was specifically highlighted to me. I knew that meant that the Holy Spirit had a message for me to give to him. In this case, it was a young guy, maybe late teens or early twenties. Now to someone in their twenties, I am an old lady in a beaten-up car, completely out of touch with the world. I am a wife and a mum of two boys, and even now am in a hurry to get home. There were no car parks as I drove by these kids and continued along the street. I was in this ongoing conversation with the Holy Spirit. I'm the one that's trying to get out of whatever it is I'm being asked to do, and he's the one encouraging me forward because he knows that this guy needs to hear what I have to say. Plus, He also knows that deep down, I want to be a world-changer that impacts people's lives, and this young person needs to know who he is. To top it off, Holy Spirit says to me, "I want you to give him some money." Now I did not have any cash on me, so giving this guy some money would mean I had to go to the bank and withdraw some cash. I am negotiating, "Ok, God, I'll do this but only if when I swing back around, number one, the guy is still there, and number two, there's a park near him where I can find the bank." True conversation. Driving to the next roundabout, I make a U-turn, winding my way back along the main street.

Lo and behold, there before me was a park; it was right in front of the ATM outside the exact bank where I have an account. Even crazier, standing right there was the guy I had a message for just hanging out talking to one of his friends. Short of a trumpet blowing and an angel appearance, what more could I have asked for. It had been made very clear that the message I had to deliver to this guy was of utmost importance. I parked, got out of my dusty beaten-up Ford Laser hatch and walked over to the ATM to withdraw some cash. All the while, this guy and his friend are watching me. I turn around and walk directly over to them; they look behind themselves, wondering who I was looking at until they realised I wanted to speak to them. I said Hi and then honed in on the young bloke who had been highlighted to me. Once again, it was a message I was there to deliver, a message of identity and hope. It was an affirmation of his sonship and a revelation of the Father's endless and undying love for him. This guy just kept on saying, "Who are you, and why are you saying this?" He was totally spinning out and completely overwhelmed by this truly left of field encounter with the Father's Love. As I finished delivering the message and began to leave, I remembered the cash. The money, I might add, that these guys watched me walk over to the ATM and withdraw from my bank. I then held out that money and gave it to them as a seal on what was spoken over this young man's life. He was speechless and simply stood there holding the cash with his mouth wide open as I jumped in my kangaroo bent car, reversed out of the parking space and drove away.

As people, we do not just 'want' to know we are worthy and valued, known and loved; we 'need' to know. It's at the core of our being, this flame, this light, this desire. Most people do not even know that it's there. Even those that do often are not living in the revelation and reality of this knowledge. Instead, we isolate ourselves and adopt an orphan mentality or an orphan spirit. We allow ourselves to rest in this place of abandonment where we align ourselves with being unwanted, unworthy and unloved. From this place, we tell ourselves that we must earn our way into the hearts of others by the things that we do. We have to deserve our place through our good performance, or we think that we must accept our plot in life and make the best of it because that's as good as it gets, and there's nothing more that can be done.

When we identify with Yeshua and understand that it is by grace[4] and not by works that we receive the Father's Love, we can then understand that we are Sons. We are the sons; I might add that all of creation is awaiting the manifestation of; it is here that we begin our journey to maturity as we come to understand that we have always had and will always be in the Father's love.

Both young men in this chapter, although I knew nothing of their lives before these encounters, were obviously living under a cloud of separation. Attached to them was an orphan spirit that was telling each of them they were fatherless, their lives were meaningless, they had no futures, and they had been forgotten. When we become love, we are then able to speak into the lives of each other in a way that only the Father of Light Himself can speak. Great news, you do not need a master's in theology to do this, nor do you need to be a pastor, a minister or a nun. You just need a willingness to be stripped back and emptied out of your personal thoughts and feelings about someone, to let subside your outwardly formed opinions about any given situation concerning them or anyone else and be willing to be filled again and again and again with the bliss and the wine of the Father's love.

Revelation – I am wonderfully and marvellously made. I am a son of the creator of the universe, and I am infinitely loved

Activation – This can be fun.
Begin an ongoing dialogue with Holy Spirit. A conversation.

Now the Holy Spirit is your friend; he is there to comfort us and to guide us by nudging us here and shining a big torch over there. He is relational; you do not have to be prim and proper; just talk like you would normally talk to anyone and wait for a response. He is able to communicate with us in the simplest and easiest ways or the wildest and most original ways you can imagine. He speaks to me in my dreams, through movies, and adverts, through the Bible and within the still quiet moments of conversation, of prayer that I have with Him in my head and my heart.

Just say Hi to Him when you wake in the morning and ask if there are any missions he has for you today. Who can you bless? How can you make a difference?

He reveals to us our beautiful Father; through the relationship with Holy Spirit, we can become ever so close to the Divine, the one with whom all things are created and made whole. We are never alone with our helper by our side.

NB: As we learn to hear His voice, you may wonder, am I getting this right? Is it God I am hearing, or is it just me? If this voice that you hear and this mission you are taking on is not founded and flowing in love, then its probably not Holy Spirit, but if it's encouraging, it builds a person up, blesses them or speaks life, love and hope over their lives then just give it a go, you have nothing to lose.

---

[4] *(Footnote: Definition via Wikipedia, the free and unmerited favour of God)

6   Intimacy with Creation's Creator.

I spoke about how I am in Him, and He is in me; this revelation is pivotal to comprehending the impossible in our world and our lives becoming possible. If I reside within the God of the universe and He resides in me, then effectively, all of creation is within me, and I am within it. That is the oneness we feel when hiking or standing outside and looking up at the clouds. It is why we love the sound of the ocean crashing on the shore or why the trickle of the waters in a creek is so soothing. It is why animals respond to us, and it's why we think of someone we haven't thought of for ages, and then they call.

When someone says 'The Universe knows' or "The Universe is always in your favour', I believe this to be true. However, it's only partially true, for if we remove the Creator of the universe from the universe herself, we are missing the foundation of where it all began. By omitting the Creator, then we omit the source of this knowing, of this greatness, the source of this power. We omit the source of this favour, this oneness and the source of this divine and complete love. You will still sense a connection; you will still have an innate sense that there is more because there is. However, while we deny that in being part of this creation, a part of this universe, we are part of the Creator Himself, we will be missing the essential ingredient that completes us, the essential piece that ultimately is the secret to this oneness. The secret to intimacy, the secret to our own truth and the secret to love.

As I began to learn more about the ways of God, of Papa, of the Divine, I began to understand more and more that His desire was to spend time with me. I had to move my understanding of Him as this big judgmental far-away fire breathing spirit to be this loving and very real, very intimate Heavenly Father. I had to go on this journey, one of discovering Him as a very mysterious and bliss-filled, crazy loving God. He had time for me and wanted to just hang out. The weird part of this was that I felt like I had to be doing something all the time, and He was just like, "chill babe, just chill". He just encouraged me over a lengthy period of time because it takes me a while to get these things, simply saying, 'Come to me, and I will give you rest, physical and mental rest'. I learned that my gateway to this intimacy was Jesus and that He, too, had time to spend with me. I have laid in those green pastures beside the bubbling brook and been overwhelmed by the peace that is found in His presence. It was a mystery to me and my middle-class upbringing that He, the Creator of the Universe, was far more concerned with my being than my doing. This gateway into His rest opened the gateway of my imagination. Hence, the wondrous gateway to the heavenly and spiritual realms filled with mystery and wonder and things beyond my wildest dreams.

There is a garden within our hearts, and it is a place where God wants to walk with us. There is too a pasture, a lush green field of dreams Yeshua wants to reveal to you; there are rivers of living water and streams of life. There are wonderful mountains of abundance and plains of discovery. There are ancient doors and pathways that open into beautiful throne rooms and tunnels and halls. This is a relationship like no other; this is a new way of living, a pathway to righteousness, and a relationship filled with connection and discovery on the highest plains. Open up your imagination, and engage with things beyond the here and now. Peace flows from the throne rooms of heaven like a river right into your everyday, into your new now.

Revelation - Being is far more powerful than doing.

Activation – Find a quiet place.
Lay down
Breathe and engage with your imagination.
Picture yourself standing in front of a big door.
As the door opens, behind it, there is a field.
A beautiful lush green field.
In the field is Jesus. He is beckoning you forward.
You enter and are surrounded by beautiful butterflies and flowers.
In the background, you hear a stream, a bubbling brook.
You can choose to lay on the beautiful green grass and look up at the sky or to swim in the bubbling brook.
There is so much peace just being here; the peace is washing over you. As you still your mind and body, and you surrender to the Prince of Peace, just breathe.
What is Jesus saying to you?

My beautiful Sister Cath passed away when she was thirty-one. Her body had been plagued with so many issues and problems stemming from a brainstem hemorrhage she had sustained several years before. In her final months on this planet, she was unable to do any of the things she had so dearly loved to do. One of those things was to run like the wind, and the other was to be in her garden and play with her children. As I was engaging with the heavens one evening, I saw my sister. She had flowers in her hair, and she was on a dancefloor in a field; she was dancing like a little girl would dance; she was dancing with Jesus. She looked so happy and so free, no longer held back by a body that did not work; it was such a gift to have seen her there in that beautiful place. I have had the joy of seeing many on the other side and have been so excited to know that as we discover more and more the realms of possibilities that are open to us, we discover the fullness of this eternal life and all that it holds whether we be in our bodies on this side or in the spirit on that. As we navigate other sides of eternity from where we stand right now, here in our natural world and our natural bodies, more and more barriers dissolve. We begin to see the fullness of who we are created to be.

"To Infinity and Beyond" – Buzz Lightyear.

7 Cleaning the Atmosphere

In 2016 my husband and I purchased an old rundown hotel in a small town in country NSW. Strangely enough, one of the most common questions when locals found out we had bought the pub was to ask us if the hotel was haunted. They would ask if we had seen ghosts or experienced anything weird. My answer was always no because I believed once we moved in there and became light in the atmosphere, all those things from the past had to leave. I was not saying that I didn't believe these strange things were real, just that they had no place in the new atmosphere that had been created upon our arrival. I had ownership here now, and that sphere of influence extends into the realms of the unseen. So, when I know who I am in the spirit, when I understand that My Father is the Father of Lights and I, as a Son or Daughter, inherit these lights, then those things that seek to cause issues and problems on my turf have no legal grounds to stay, they must leave. If you notice, when you walk into a dark room, and you turn on the light, the darkness has to leave, for there is no place for darkness in the light.

I always do a 'walk through' when we arrive in a new home. I announce that the atmosphere is being cleaned and cleared of everything that has chosen to fill this space. The space is now being filled with the atmosphere of heaven, with the goodness of Yeshua, with the blood of Jesus. I release Angels into the rooms, the hallways and the surrounding precinct, and I cast my Shalom like a shadow over the area. Now it's interesting that many people commented, "We have noticed that it feels different on your corner of the street now" they mentioned that it felt lighter and that people feel a general sense of happiness when they come inside. It just feels good.

If we are to have freedom in our lives, we cannot be held back by fears and disturbances from the past, especially when they are not ours to hold onto. If these spirits and presences in our homes and workplaces are left over from others who have once been here and are now gone or perhaps not gone, then when we as children of light come into these spaces, these things have no right to stay. In any of the places we live and move, we have authority. In these places of authority, these ghosts, vibes, spirits, whatever you choose to call them, they cannot stay. However, if you do not know who rules in your life and you are allowing yourself to just blow in the wind, susceptible to whatever stuff happens to blow in, then this is where we open ourselves up to all kinds of outside forces and unknown things. In recognising that we are infinitely powerful, we must also recognise where the source of our power comes from. In turn, we need to understand how and where other things may have access to us.

Ian Clayton, an author and businessman from New Zealand, has put together this diagram of the gateways; it's especially good to have a picture of these access points so we can better understand the ways in which we give access to things in our outside word and how these things may affect our thought patterns, our speech and dictate to us though our passions and fears. At the very centre is the first love gate; it is the fullness of our revelation of His love for us.

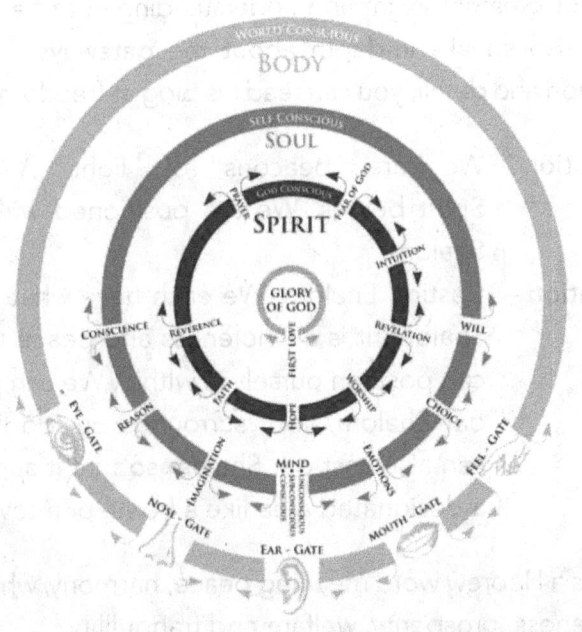

This diagram is retrieved from freedomarc.blog and is based on a diagram by Ian Clayton (sonofthunder.org).

The part I love about this is once we have a revelation of God's love for us, once I understand that the Creator of the Universe wants to dwell within me. This revelation flows through every other piece of my being. When we have this revelation of love, the abuses, regrets and misdemeanours of our past may rear their ugly head. Still, they cannot take control of those areas of our life ever again. Our first love gate is in the centre of our being, in our spirit and its untouchable; we may have locked it up or closed it down, but it can be reopened, and the living water that flows out of the restoration of relationship and the revelation of love, can freely flow.

Ian speaks in-depth in his book Realms of the Kingdom Volume 1 about the Gateways. I would recommend this to you if you are looking for greater insight and understanding in this area. Mike Parsons also speaks in-depth about the gateways. For more information and detail, you can read his blog at freedomarc.blog

Revelation – We are beacons of light. We are Spirit beings. We are positioned within the Shalom.

Activation – Casting Shalom. We each have what we call Shalom; it is a wholeness and peace that we can position ourselves within. We can puff up our Shalom, so it surrounds our bodies; we can also cast our Shalom so that it surrounds a designated area like a home or a town.

Shalom is a Hebrew word meaning peace, harmony, wholeness, completeness, prosperity, welfare and tranquillity.

8 Out of this world.

From a young age, the spirit world was very real to me. I have always had this knowing that I was created for something more and that the more was something more real than everything I could see. I now understand that this extends far beyond my wildest imagination, and believe me, I have a very wild imagination. Our influence extends to governance in many spheres of life. Our influence extends to many regions of our city and nation, our galaxy, planet and universe. This governance and authority can all be executed in the realm of the spirit.

I grew up in country Australia. As a farmer's daughter, I developed a special connection with the land and all those things that grew on it, crops, plants, flowers and trees. I knew what it was to have the wind in my hair as I rode through the wide-open spaces on horses and bikes, what it was like to feel the breath of freedom as I climbed trees and hiked hills. I spent countless hours in the great outdoors. Still, to this day, the wilderness, the mountains, the sunset and sunrise, the birdsong and the expanse of the desert plains remain places of spirit connection and Zen for me. I also became aware during these formative years how greatly affected we as humans are by those things that were understood to be out of our control. The greatest and the most impacting of these on our lives and livelihoods as people of the land appeared to be the weather.

The weather, with all its goodness, also has the potential to wreak havoc in our lives, leaving a trail of uncontrollable devastation. We need the rain, it's essential. However, we do not want it to rain too much; fussy, I know, but we don't want flooding, and we certainly don't want drought.

Now I get it that things like the weather seem out of our control but what if they are not. You see, from a Spiritual perspective, with Jesus being my spirit guide, He did this thing while he walked the earth, a miracle of sorts that appeared to be just everyday life for Him. In the midst of raging seas, he stretched out His arms, and he calmed the storm. He also said, "I tell you this timeless truth: The person who follows me in faith, believing in me, will do the same miracles that I do – even greater miracles than these..."(John 14:12). My understanding is that Jesus did some crazy cool stuff in his three and a half years of ministry on the earth. One of which was governing the weather.

This leads me to question our ineffectiveness in dealing with the weather patterns and wonder if the power within me can influence the power in the world. So, I set about a lifelong journey of discovering if and how this might be possible. There was already a knowing that while ever I was within creation herself that I felt different, that I could speak to the trees and the mountains, and there was a strange sense of response. I began to hear of others who were experiencing similar encounters and were connecting to the Creator in the midst of creation. I believed in the power of prayer and felt that my prayers were impacting the things around me; I also believed in the power of positive thinking and positive declarations and was seeing these bring transformation in my life. I had a hope and an expectation for the future and the good things that it held. I still felt that all of this left me in a state where I was not as powerful as I had expected, and I was not seeing the results I believed were possible. I was not seeing too much beyond the imaginable. My desire was to live within the unimaginable, the inconceivable and the impossible. After all, He Himself lived within me, and He had spoken it into being and given it all life in the first place.

I began to practice my thoughts beyond just prayer. So instead of just praying prayers like, 'Lord, we need rain, please make it rain', I began to speak to the clouds, to the weather patterns, I began to call into being those things that were not as though they were. Essentially, I began to use the power in my mouth to activate the faith within my heart to see these things together culminate in a fruitful and constructive weather system. I began to engage with the elementals.

We were camping on the mid-north coast of NSW, this was many years ago now, and a storm was brewing offshore. It was immense; the clouds were black and green, the wind was blustery, and the rumbling thunder was ferociously rolling towards us. I thought to myself, if I am to see this storm subside, then I best make my way out to that rocky headland and speak to it. If I am to begin this weather whispering journey, I must begin somewhere, and this felt like a Jesus moment to me, so off I went. A cold change was blowing in, there wasn't a person to be seen, and the rain was hitting my face. I kept praying and walking. As I reached the headland right out on the rocks beside the crashing waves and the deep dark ocean, I began speaking to the storm.

Strangely enough, the storm was speaking back to me with a ferocious boom and a face full of rain. I kept it up for a while as the storm closed in and completely soaked me through. I wandered back to the campsite with a strange sense of excitement like there was more to this than I could ever have imagined. I passed a guy walking the beach. The Holy Spirit gave me a word of encouragement for him, which I passed on; it spun him out; I love that about God. He is in everything, and He is a complete spin out. My words projected into the stratosphere; they didn't stop the storm, so why tell the story? What is my point? The point is that we are beginning to open the door of possibility; we are daring to believe that through us, things can change. We are practising, honing and releasing our faith to see the immeasurable, faith that knocks on the door of the impossible and invites it into the realms of possibility into the reality of our lives.

This is the day that the Lord has made, and we will rejoice and be glad in it. We are standing on the brink of a New Now. A New Way of doing things, a new operating system, a new way of seeing and moving and creating. We must press into Him, the Mysterious and all-knowing One, for the keys to open up the possibilities held within our future. That day on the rocky outcrop in the midst of the storm, I could have been disappointed; I could have concluded this stuff was not real. Rome wasn't built in a day, nor will I ever comprehend the goodness that is stored up for me in the heavenly places, the downloads, the governance, the angel armies; how will I ever know what could be possible if I just give up at the very beginning. I remember listening to a testimony given by Todd White, a wild Jesus lover and evangelist. He spoke of praying for over 900 people, one by one over many months before finally he saw one of these people get healed. He now sees hundreds of people healed every year as he prays. Still, if he had given up after the first disappointment, he would never have stepped into the fullness of everything that he was created to be. He is now living in the impossible, and miracles are now what he sees; they are his reality.

I could see heaven cheering me on that afternoon as I got soaked by that storm. I could see the cloud of witnesses excited that I was having a go; they were excited that I had gone from believing that it was possible to standing out there on that headland and putting my conviction into practice. The storm did not subside; it did not retreat, but neither did I, and I am still here to talk about it today.

Since that day, I have had many experiences and encounters with the weather. Some have turned out how I would have imagined, and some have not. I may never know the fullness of what I had taken part in, but I know that while we have the Father's heart for this world, the more we become who we were created to be. The more creation, the more nature responds to us, and the more she will come into the fullness of herself. The more we understand who we are and how we are intended to engage with everything around us, the more restoration we will see in that sphere of our world. Sometimes it looks as though Mother Nature is imploding. It looks as though the effects of our misuse of her and her resources and the very goodness she provides us with have brought us to a place where we cannot go back. When we look at the rainforests, the reefs, and the oceans that we are custodians of, our lack of responsibility and understanding of our role in caring for these places have merely manifested destruction. I believe this is only due to us not understanding our role as sons and daughters on the earth. As caretakers we have not understood who we are and therefore have thought that the restoration of this world is completely out of our hands, that we are headed down a one-way track and there ain't no coming back. We must understand that we are powerful agents of change, so that negative doom and gloom thinking couldn't be further from the truth.

It has been scientifically proven that we emit a frequency and a sound as part of our being, and this frequency impacts the things around us. In a simplistic form, you would know that if someone were to walk into a room and they are giving off a negative vibe, the other people around them can feel it. This frequency and sound are part of the restoration that we are partnering in. Mike Parsons from Freedom Arc in the UK says, "We use the creative power of our consciousness to create reality. We do it all the time, most of us unintentionally! If you want things to be different, you have to make intentional choices…" (Mike Parsons – Expanding our Reality Intensive).

I love the way Mike frames up for us this incredible potential that we hold as sons and daughters that we are continuing to discover and step into. He says, "As sons of God, we should expect our mental abilities to be far superior to those we currently enjoy. It is our framework of belief that creates that limitation"- Mike Parsons freedomarc.blog.

And do not be conformed to this world but be transformed by the renewing of your mind (Rom 12:2)

There is a huge increase in the way we are engaging with nature and the world around us. It is the crazy ones on the fringes of our culture that seem to be most likely to step into these things first. If we think our education systems, with their rigid conformity, are the ones to embrace this new way of thinking and to equip us with the skills and knowledge first and to walk out into this wild, crazy life with its unknown and unpredictable ways, then we are kidding ourselves.

I recently attended a yoga and sound river retreat where the facilitators of this retreat were constantly engaging with nature and all that she is and represents. They are speaking to the trees, the waters, and the skies; they understood that there is a spiritual connection between us and nature. That we, as part of this creation, are intrinsically woven into one another and into the world around us. How are we, as Christians missing this? How are we, as wilderness warriors missing this? How are we completely ignoring our responsibility and the honour that we are created for in this space? To govern and to caretake this wonder and beauty held within the realm of nature and of creation herself.

For all creation is waiting, yearning for the time when the children of God will be revealed. You see, all of creation has collapsed into emptiness, not by its own choosing, but by God's. Still, He placed within it a deep and abiding hope that creation would one day be liberated from its slavery to corruption and experience the glorious freedom of the children of God. For we know that all creation groans in unison with birthing pains up until now (Rom 8:19-22 VOI)

Justin Paul Abraham says in His book 'Beyond Human' that creation has a "deep and abiding hope" for you to learn your relationship with it and to see it free. I realise we've barely begun to understand that. ... As 'Kainos' Sons, perhaps it's time for us to realise we are made to join God's creative initiative and help nature (Kainos comes from ancient Greek and means 'New' or 'Fresh').

The prophet Bob Jones used to say that we are shields of the earth. That it is our job to help protect the earth from disaster.

After one look at this planet, any visitor from outer space would say, 'I want to see the manager'" – William S Burroughs.

Artist and Professor at Cornwell university Andy Goldsworthy is quoted as saying, "We often forget that we are nature. Nature is not something separate from us. So, when we say we have lost our connection to nature, we have lost our connection to ourselves."

We must understand as spiritual beings and lovers of God that there are many people out there in the world that are recognising their power and place long before we are. They are stepping into realms of possibility far beyond the realms that we as Christians are currently living in. We must wake up, we must stand up, we must be who we were created to be. We are standing in the unfolding of a great awakening. We must take hold of the freedom that is ours; we must be responsible custodians of our land; we must be lovers of all creation, one another, and the world around us. We must be filled with gratitude, and our hearts must be filled with the transforming love of the Father. We must begin to open ourselves up 'to the impossible, the invisible, the mystical, and the fruits of everything we thought had passed and was no longer ours will become the way we live and move and have our being on earth. If we are to see creation fully restored and people fully set free, if we are to see our fellow man-made whole and experience true love, then we must understand who we are and begin to live out of this revelation. We ourselves are free; we must be wild lovers, fully engaged with the divine nature of God being fully present here and there all at the same time.

> Blessed are the peacemakers, for they will be called sons of God (Matthew, 5:9).

> For [even the whole] creation [all nature] waits eagerly for the children of God to be revealed. (Rom 8:19 AMP).

> For the shields of the earth belong to God (psalms 47:9 NKJV).

> Earths Guardians Belong to God (Psalms 47:9, CEB).

We have an incredible privilege to navigate the crossing over space. That space between the seen and unseen realms. It's exciting and filled with mystery; we also have a guide who takes our hand and shows us the way. Holy Spirit, our friend, our counsellor, our confidant. The one who laughs with us and cries with us, comforts us and empowers us, breathes fire into and pours rain over us all at the same time. He is mystery and clarity and wonder and truth all in the same breath. Jesus is our friend, Yeshua, our brother, our lover and our miracle-working God. He is the doorway to the heavens, the one we enter all of eternity through. He is the way to our Father. He is the truth; He is Life, and He is our saviour, the liberator of mankind. Yod-Heh-Vav-Heh (YHVH), Our Father, our beautiful Papa, our wondrous and mighty God. Yahweh, emblazoned with light and Love. So fierce are His affections for us, so wild is His desire to be with us and us to be with Him. So desperately, He longs for communion, fellowship, and endless feasting at His banquet table, set for a King, a Daughter, a Son. Within them, there are three. Within them, there is a unity and oneness that completes us. It is an example of the beautiful unity and oneness we are to be on the earth. It is the difference and the sameness all at once. It's separate, but together, it's three, and it's one. Together we can have a profound impact; we can do so much together.

On this journey, I have found so many others who have been

tasked with our guidance and help, with our friendship and companionship. Wisdom, with her flowing blonde hair and her beautiful white dresses, King David with his dashing good looks and his raw heart of love for the Father, the great cloud of witnesses and the millions upon millions of heavenly hosts, angels and ancient ones. The ones that have gone before and those who remain and have never crossed over. There is still so much for us to understand. It's sooooo incredibly exciting!!

Live consistent with who you really are, inspired by the loving-kindness of God. Do not allow current religious tradition to mould you into its pattern of reasoning. Live an inspired artist, give attention to the detail of God's desire to find expression in you. Become acquainted with perfection. To accommodate yourself to the delight and good pleasure of him will transform your thoughts afresh from within (Romans 12:1-2, Mirror Bible).

Don't become so well-adjusted to your culture that you fit into it without even thinking. Instead, fix your attention on God. You'll be changed from the inside out. Readily recognise what he wants from you and quickly respond to it. Unlike the culture around you, always dragging you down to its level of immaturity, God brings the best out in you, develops well-formed maturity in you (Romans 12:2, Message Bible).

Aligning our thoughts with His thoughts. Aligning our thoughts with God's thoughts about us, His good thoughts. I know, right? God has GOOD THOUGHTS about us. So when we begin to see ourselves as He sees us, from a place of love, restoration and a renewed mind, from that place we begin to live and walk and see one another and everything around us with beautiful new eyes, we begin to see everything differently.

Revelation – All of creation, all of nature is awaiting the revealing of the sons of God….

Activation – Get up close and personal with nature. Take a walk in the forest, by the river or through the parklands. Just allow yourself to experience and feel the breeze on your skin, to see the movement of the leaves in the trees. Speak to them if you feel brave enough and watch for them to speak back.

I have planted many vegetable gardens over the years. I am not a horticulturist, and I know little of the scientific names or applications of plants. I have, however, grown vegetables in areas where long term residents to that area have told me I would not be able to grow them or if I did, they would be eaten by grubs. I have not used chemicals and have just grown my plants with water, weeding and love. I have been light in their midst, sung the occasional song and had many a conversation in the spirit as I have tended to that piece of ground in my care. Those plants have produced delicious, nourishing fruit and vegetables in return, and it has been a joy to have been part of the process, which is like a circle.

Revelation – I come alive outside

Activation – Plant some veggies or flowers and spend time with them. Speak life over them and feel the frequency of the life-giver in you emanating out onto all surrounding you. It's good for the soul.

9 The Sound of Silence

There is something ever so powerful about being able to sit in that place of silence. You might call it meditation, contemplation or the secret place. Yes, it is hard to find in our busy world, and it's confronting, especially with all those thoughts going around and around in my head. The question presents itself, yes, the one that speaks of being ok with my own company. We are all wired differently, and for many of us, the sounds of silence are deafening

Our society and culture have become increasingly loud, busy and demanding. Even if we do find a quiet place for a while, our ears will be ringing with the remnants of our day, and our minds will be buzzing back and forth from one idea or scenario to the next. As I pull back from this busyness, contemplating what may be on the other side of the silence that I seek, I find myself reaching for my phone or fighting back feelings of fruitlessness. In my quest for that place of peace and serenity, I battle with my mind as it tells me there are things to get done, a house to tidy, work to attend to. It is also the voice that whispers to me that this pursuit of silence is an ineffective and wasteful use of my time.

Silence is an ancient path to enlightenment. Many religions and cultures across our planet practice in some form this silence. It may be the practice of contemplation, meditation or prayer. It may be just a little or perhaps a complete immersion as in the monastic life. It is here in this place of surrender that we lose ourselves, and we connect with the spirit. Here, we find our God and the wonder and mystery of all that is life. The wonder in this is simply in losing oneself; we find oneself, just stripped of this busyness, stripped of the analyzing and the round and around and around in our mind. We are laid bare and emptied, ready to be filled again with all that has been laid up for us from the beginning of time, all that life, all that goodness, that bliss and that wine of His love. To be filled with an awareness of the revelation, the mystery and the love of the Creator of the universe. In our sacrificial action of zipping the mind and the lip, we open ourselves up to the impossible in our lives. Is that too much? Have I lost you on this mystical journey of attaining something beyond the rational thoughts of our mind? Have I lost you when I alluded to none of this having to make sense?

Are we there yet? Well, I'm getting there. Like every new way forward, it takes some time to create a habit, and the practice of this place of silence for me is often sporadic. I have spent whole years in scheduled prayer, in meditation and in the secret place. That quiet place I take myself away to, so I can just completely immerse myself in the presence of the Holy Spirit, in the presence of God. That place is my connection with spirit, where I ascend into the realms of possibility beyond the here and now, things beyond myself. As the years progressed, I have felt at times that it has been nearly impossible to carve out the smallest moment of quiet in my life's non-stop, hectic days. It is from this place of perpetual busyness I have learned that I am continuously positioned IN Him and Him in me. Therefore, I do not need to whisk myself away to a quiet place. However, I do still love that because, effectively, I am living from a seat of continual rest. This place of rest is found in the centre of Jesus, which is where I am, as He is in me, and I am in Him.

Yes, it's that wondrous place I have mentioned previously. That place of Bliss that springboards you into a place of revelation about how truly close we are to God if we really want to step into Him.

So back to the silence, the meditation, the bliss that is found within that place. Why bring it up? Why is it important? Why is it a thing? Would it just be better to be the hands and feet to be 'doing' this thing called love? Absolutely yes, this is super important. However, we must be doing it from a place of rest.

The body is a great reservoir of wisdom. Something as simple as bodily stillness and breathing makes a contribution of untold value to discovering the unfathomable silence deep within us. This silence, as RS Thomas tells us in " ÄD" in collected Later Poems, "is when we live in listening distance to the silence we call God" (Into the Silent Land – Martin Laird).

As we try to attain this place of silence, of meditation, where we move beyond ourselves, our thoughts and into that place in the spirit realm, we can find numerous distractions. I have used music, Bible verses and even what is called the prayer word to bring myself into that place of engagement, of letting go, that place of bliss and beyond. The anonymous author of 'The Cloud of Unknowing' suggests you just say one word. "Take only a short word of only one syllable; that is better than one of two syllables, for the shorter it is, the better it agrees with the work of the spirit. A word of this kind is the word God or the word Love, choose whichever you wish or another if you please, whichever you prefer of one syllable and fasten this word to your heart so that it never parts from it, whatever happens."

His book 'Into the Silent Land', Martin Laird states that the prayer word is something like a vaccination; a small dose of the disease in question is introduced to the patient to call forth those antibodies that will ultimately ward off the disease. In this case, the disease in question is the overactive mind, which is undeniably important in many of life's tasks, obscures the deeper ground of being and leaves us with the sense that we are separate from God and others.

Here's a little story of one such occasion several years ago where I found myself on the other side of this contemplative, sitting in rest, meditative prayer. It's a little taste of what is on the other side and how crazy it can be when we just let go and step in.

Journal Entry 2015 - 'WOW, where do I begin? I never know how much to tell about what goes on in my life on any given day, for if you followed me with a video camera for 24hrs, you would not even see the half of it. This journey of discovering the extent of what is out there in the supernatural realms and what I have access to as a son, a daughter of our infinite and ever-living God, is MIND BLOWING. Last week I travelled to the mid-north coast of NSW, Australia, on an invitation from a friend and a word from God. I knew I needed to be there, it was a totally last moment trip, and I spent 18 hrs driving in the car and just 16 waking hours on the coast. As I was driving toward the city where I was to stay, I could hear Papa, my heavenly Father, whispering, "this is our time". I was totally expectant for next level encounters with heaven, with the angels and the saints of old, with beautiful Jesus and my Papa Daddy, my beautiful Heavenly Father, Creator of the universe, with God. I arrived just before 10pm after an incredible 10 hr journey filled with revelation and teaching, singing, counsel and love poured straight out from heaven. I knew I had to begin with communion, and as I checked in, I discovered room service stopped at 10pm, so I headed straight for the kitchen. Bread rolls? Yes, and a piccolo bottle of wine; I was totally peaking.

I sat in my room feasting in faith on the blood and body of my Jesus. As He began transforming me, changing me and sanctifying me, I began to fully come into His glorious presence.

I put on some music; Mark Steen, a crazy amazing songwriter whose music fully shifts you in a completely reconfiguring kind of way, was my choice for the evening. With that, I opened the word... His Word and I SAT right in the middle of Psalm 23.

Entering in, that is what I wanted so desperately to do, but not like I ever had before. I have had dreams and seen visions, I have been outside my body and watched what was happening in the room, I have encountered angels and by faith stood in the Courts of Heaven, I have travelled in my dreams, but I wanted to SEE on another level, I wanted to enter into the reality of heaven like I never had before. I want to walk in other dimensions with my body; I wanted to walk on other parts of our earth.

Engaging with my spirit man, where that part of me was becoming more real than the pieces I could see with my earthly eyes, I meditated on Psalm 23. I wanted there to be an after, a follow on to the frame I had framed up in my imagination, an end to the piece of the story I had begun. Still, I would not know what it was until I had fully stepped in. I wanted to have an encounter that was as real as my dreams but to have it while I was still awake. Praise Jesus, this would be it. This psalm, Psalm 23, was my prayer word, my door. As I sat in it, meditating on every word, piece by piece, this beautiful psalm became my gateway, my entry point and just like that, I stepped through.

BOOOM....... I was falling, down, down, down; I was in a huge expanse of glittery blue water; it was like aquamarine jelly. It was very thick, and I was totally immersed in it. I felt like I should have been completely freaking out because I was surrounded and locked in. For someone who tends to be a little claustrophobic, this is not my favourite feeling, but my beautiful Jesus He had me. He reassured me I could breathe underwater, and I could. I knew this was my stepping in, and I couldn't wait to discover more of the mystery; not only was I underwater, I was breathing, and I was totally cool with it.

Suddenly just like that, I was in China. I have travelled in the nighttime hours, in the dreamtime before. I had visited many places across the globe. Although this experience was similar, there was another level of reality about it this time. As I travelled, there were three specific parts to the journey. I was in a boat with some people, and we were talking. When I left the boat, I left pieces of my belongings; then, I was in a car, and we were talking. When I got out of the car once again, I left pieces of my belongings. Finally, I was walking through the streets, and it occurred to me that I had left my phone and all the other things I needed in the places I had already been. Thoughts began to race through my mind, 'what If I needed to call for help? How will I be able to? What if I was cold or hungry or in trouble?' then I heard Jesus say, "I am with you. I will not forsake you; I am and will supply EVERYTHING you need." CRAZY!!!

So even though I am in the spirit, a place where He has brought me, I still freak out that I don't have all that I might need. It's laughable to me that He continues to have to reassure me that He is everything and gives everything to me for all that He calls me to do. Even as we walk the heavenly landscape together and travel to places across the globe, He still reassures me of my need to operate out of this place of rest in Him. Can I really trust this guy? I believe the answer is, Yes, I can.

So, what do we make of all this? I mean, do you even have a grid that this can go on? I have, for my entire life, wondered about what the 'more' was. I always felt like I was created for 'more'. As I have travelled through the last 40 plus years, I have been unable to find this 'more' in any kind of achievement or success. I have not found it in relationships or children, nor have I found it in substances, church, or career. I have only been able to find this place deep in the very heart of my Father, of my God. HIS RICHES, HIS GLORY. I have discovered that My God will supply (fill to the full) my every need according to HIS riches, IN Glory, IN Christ Jesus. When I am IN Him, and He is IN me, then I begin to go the way that I was destined to go before the beginning of time. It's then that I begin to discover what is this 'more'.

As I awoke the next morning, I could see that Philippians 4:19 was to be my gateway. In my journeys the night before, I was going in one direction, and my stuff, as I left it behind, was going in the other direction. As I left behind pieces of the things I no longer needed, then my hands began to be free, and I could then hold the hand of the one who would lead me. He was beckoning me to take His hand and to not let go. Woah!

EVERYTHING is not as it seems, my beautiful friends. I urge you to step out of your comfort zone, out of that place where we must have all the answers and dive headfirst into heaven's mysteries. I urge you to step into the mysteries of a realm that we do not need to die to have access to. I recommend wholeheartedly for you to jump into the wonder and the love of the arms of a Father who just longs to sit with you and look into your eyes. A Father who knows every thought in your mind and every hair on your head. You are powerful, and discovering WHO YOU REALLY ARE, rather than what you need to do, is the beginning of an incredible adventure that will last a long and wonder-filled lifetime. It will last into eternity. It is time to move on; your life is calling...... JESUS is calling you. He is the doorway to adventure and wonder and Bliss. He is the doorway to your 'more-way'.

Revelation – The door is in the floor. His name is Jesus; Jesus is your door to more.

Activation – Surrender all!! A wonderful activation that I did when I was running with the discovery of this concept of just jumping in, letting go and loosening up, not being so serious all the time. I was visiting a friend of mine, and I just ran out into her backyard fully clothed and jumped into the pool. It was liberating, silly, hilarious and crazy all at once. It made no sense to do it, but that is why I had to. It was breaking off the sensible, the normal, the proper and the civilized. It was embracing the undignified, the crazy, the wild and the free. It was opening up a world of possibility.

10 Divine Health and Immortality

This topic is very close to my heart; controversial, yes, but what emerging solution to something currently unsolvable isn't a little out there. Seriously who wouldn't like to tap into the fountain of eternal youth, drink the elixir of everlasting life and never be sick or wrinkled again?

Like many others, I had heard stories and testimonies of the miraculous healings that were going on around the world. I would often rise before the sun to watch healing evangelists on early morning television, back before we could tune in and watch on-demand. I was fascinated by the enormity of what was possible. It made so much sense to me that illnesses and diseases were not meant to be a part of us or a part of our world. There was one thing, however, that kept me at arm's length from praying in this way, and that was I just had not experienced any of these wild out-there miracles for myself, nor did I know anyone that had either.

When my sister Cath was twenty-six, she had a brain stem hemorrhage akin to a stroke. I mentioned her just briefly in a previous chapter. This was something that just did not happen to people her age. She was married with two gorgeous little girls and was incredibly independent. She was a doer who loved farm life, gardening and the arts. So, when this freak medical episode happened to her, it was devastating for our family; we all felt completely unprepared to deal with it. I remember that first visit after we found out that she had been flown to an intensive care unit in Sydney. When we arrived, the nursing staff only let us go into ICU in twos. So, one of my sisters and I went in together. We were completely ill-prepared for what we were going to see and the raw and intense emotion that was going to come out of that visit. Cath was hooked up to so many tubes and monitors it was like something out of the movies. She was in an induced coma; we were told to say our goodbyes as they were not sure if she would make it through till the morning. There were a whole bunch of doctors there, and it would seem they were deliberating over what to do.

It's one of those unenviable scenarios when things are completely out of your hands. I had no medical training. Nor did anyone else in our immediate family; we were unable to help at all. Her life was in the hands of the medical professionals, so we prayed. When I say we prayed, we didn't just pray; we rallied everyone from everywhere to pray. Schools were praying, churches were praying, grannies in their homes and friends on their commute to work were all praying. We were collectively crying out for this miraculous working God to step into her circumstances and do the unimaginable. We desperately wanted her to survive; we wanted her to live.

I believe that night Cath did get her miracle, although that too could be debated, she did not rise up from her bed and walk out of the hospital, but she was alive. She had no movement from the neck down, and slowly over the course of the next couple of weeks, she recovered enough to be transferred from ICU onto the general neurological ward. It was a slow process; she had become a young woman trapped inside an old person's body. It was an arduous journey as, over the coming months and years, she learned to walk, talk and move all over again. It took months and months and months of intensive rehabilitation, and even then, she never completely recovered. It was a miracle to have her with us at all, and we were grateful for that. She went on to have another baby, a beautiful boy. Considering the high concentration of drugs in her system during everything that had transpired over those previous few years, a baby was a miracle in itself. Then the unimaginable happened, there were complications, and she hemorrhaged again.

This time she needed major surgery. We were ever hopeful that this surgery would take her back to complete wholeness, back where she was before any of this ever happened; the doctors were hopeful for this too. Sadly, for Cath, her beautiful husband and three children, that surgery was the beginning of an agonizing eight months her body dragged itself through before she finally passed away. I remember that call I received from her husband telling me it was almost over. I cried out in that moment, 'Heal her, God, we want her back completely whole and if you can't do that, then take her so she doesn't have to suffer this trauma anymore'.

Cath's husband called again some hours later to inform us of her passing.... I was devastated, shocked, sad, and so angry. I was so mad at myself that I hadn't made more time for her, mad at God because my sister dying was the wrong answer to a heartfelt prayer. We wanted her whole; we wanted her healed. But I also felt that she didn't want to be suffering anymore; she didn't want to be helpless and decrepit. She just wanted to go home. She wanted to be free.

It took me many months, even years, to fully embrace God again after that. I was lost in a sea of distress and grief. As much as I knew where she now was, was so much better than what her life had become, I just felt like she'd all been ripped off. I had spent my whole life believing anything was possible, and yet here was an impossible situation that it seemed no amount of faith could do anything about. It's another mystery that makes so much more sense when we see things with an eternal perspective. After seeing her dancing with Jesus, there is not a piece of me that doubts she is in a wonderful place and that freedom truly exists beyond the brokenness and sickness of our world.

I could have let this disappointment, anger, sadness and devastation put a stop to any thoughts of miracles, to any notion of God being a part of my life ever again. I could have just stopped moving forward into Him, and I did for a time. However, this testimony is all part of the Mystery, the unanswered questions; it has a part within those things we are yet to understand. These experiences are part of a bigger picture than the one we can currently see. From the ridiculously small box of our lives, we can't possibly comprehend nor see properly the fullness of what is on the outside, what is beyond.

It's been over 10 years since my sister went to be with Jesus. I had that beautiful vision of her dancing on heaven's dance floor; she looked so young and so beautiful, and more than anything else, she looked so free. She was free from that body that had been crippled by sickness. She was free to dance and play and run and sing. Even now, I smile as I remember her dry sense of humour, her cruisy attitude and her simplistic approach to life. I smile because I know, in a strange way, she was healed when she left us, just not in the way we sought nor completely understood at the time.

So, this brings me to the present, where I can see that I have moved on from angry to ok to picking up where I left off over the past ten or so years. I have then advanced even further to leaving behind everything I had ever been taught or read about healing and wholeness. I am now learning ways and being activated in truths that I would never have imagined I would have been a part of nor believed a few short years ago. It is completely new to me; it's ancient, but it's new. An ancient technology that is being seen in a different light.

As I have sat with my Yahweh in the Heavenly places these past twelve or so years, he has taught me things that I had previously not known nor understood. He has revealed truths and encouraged me to partake in practices and activations that have seen divine health, healing, and wholeness become my reality. A reality that I had only ever dreamt could be real.

I have been so blessed to have found others too, who have been on a similar path and have gleaned from their encounters and experience. These wonderful ones have spurred me on; they have encouraged me and made me realise that I am not crazy, there are lots of us out there, and we are seeing a very new, very real way forward in our lives and our world. Together we are framing up a New Now.

In August 2018, I attended a conference just outside Melbourne, Australia. It was mind-blowing. It was also pivotal. I spent a large portion of that weekend completely smashed by the drunken bliss of the Holy Spirit. I was legless on His wine, His love like I had never been before. To get a little perspective on this, at the time, I was a publican's wife. In the Hotel Industry in Australia, we have an industry standard, which is a professional set of rules outlining those things we are responsible for. One of which is the responsible service of alcohol. The short of it is, we don't let people get legless when they drink. This weekend in Melbourne, I had not drunk a drop of alcohol; I was, however, completely undone. I was intoxicated on the Wine of His Presence, on the Wine of His Love. I had been whacked by the joy of His goodness and was making a bit of a scene about it, completely unintentional, but for anyone that has been around a drunk person, that's what they do.

For the previous six or so years, I had been very active in the realms of the spirit. I had retreated from most forms of public worship, prayer and public gatherings. I had been spending a lot of time receiving revelation and teaching on everything from The Order of Melchizedek to The Government of Heaven and the mysteries held in the myriad of halls and rooms where I would be led to visit each time I ascended into the heavenly realms. It sounds so out of this world, but this multidimensional life was becoming my norm. I had spent so much time there that there was just no going back for me.

As Godfrey Birtill so eloquently put in his fabulous song 'We've Gone (Beep Beep).'

> 'We've gone so far out that we can't go back.
>
> Beep, Beep! Beep Beep!
>
> It's a one-way ticket up the ancient track.
>
> Beep, Beep! Beep, Beep!
>
> Can't go back to building empire
>
> Can't go back to behind the barbed wire

Can't go back to a dampened fire now
Can't go back to boring meetings
Can't go back to pop chart singing
Can't go back we're off adventuring now.
We'd just had enough and got on this bus. To Glorious Jesus!
Can't go back to hierarchy
Can't go back to the 'in-crowd' parties
Can't go back to that malarkey now
Can't go back to dead religion
Can't go back to being driven
Can't go back we've tasted heaven now.

I have gone so far out with this; I have walked in the wilderness; I then sat in the quiet places with Holy Spirit as he has taught me over many years about this road that we were to go on.

I was going deep on many levels, all the while the healing and wholeness portion of this journey was one that I had just left up there on the shelf. I knew that I was being led right into the fullness of new revelation in this space; I had a knowing that I was going to see the impossible become my possible; it just was not that time.

A conference I had attended in New Zealand the year before had really kicked it off, as one of the presenters there had shared a teaching on loving our bodies. It was such a wonderful confirmation of direction, another piece of the puzzle that played a big part in this book, this teaching and moving forward in this space of divine health and wholeness. I was being reminded that it was a big piece on this journey to being healed and free. It fitted in with so many things I had worked through in my twenties, things about self-worth and acceptance. But there was another level we were beginning to tap into; it was more powerful.

In Melbourne, Nancy Coen had shared about being clothed in Divine Heath and Immortality. Along with those positive declarations of love that we speak over our bodies, I began to clothe myself daily in this new outfit. Divine Health and Immortality were what I now slipped on every morning as I dressed, just like one would put on a jacket or a shawl. After departing this retreat, I felt a renewed sense of empowerment. I had received so much confirmation for many of the things Papa had been revealing to me over the past years. I had received further framework, an enlarged capacity, and I had been rocked by the drunken wine of His love.

As I journeyed home, I was filled with hope for the future. It looked bright, although still filled with impossible situations; there was a quiet optimism within me. I was excited to see the impossible turn into some kind of new reality.

On returning, I had a strange growth removed from my face and not long after, it was diagnosed as cancer. How was this happening? Why was this happening? Cancer was not the hope-filled future that I had envisaged. It was November, and I was booked to have the cancer removed by a surgeon in Sydney in February. What initially seemed like an eternity away was upon us before we knew it. I was scheduled to attend my post-operative appointment just two days before the operation. During the confirmation process, the surgery phoned to inform me that my health fund was not covering the cost of the operation. I would have to pay the full amount on admission to the hospital on the morning of my surgery. It was just over seven thousand dollars in just three days' time.

I swallowed hard, and my heart sank. Ordinarily, with a little juggling, this would have been possible. However, our region was in the middle of one of the worst droughts on record, and business was not exactly booming. We had no extra money for this operation. There were no spare funds sitting in some mysterious emergency account, just waiting there for such an occasion as this. There was no other choice; I had to postpone the surgery.

I have to admit, I was a little concerned. I didn't like the fact that there was cancer on my face, and it needed to be removed, and because of a trivial thing like money, it wasn't able to be. The next availability they had for me was June. As the months rolled by, I had been actively targeting this cancer each morning as I declared over myself, 'I am clothed in Divine Health and Immortality.' I had also been engaging with Communion.

Now I understand that in most churches, Communion is taken in remembrance of what Jesus has done for us. The Holy sacraments remind us that Jesus died on the cross for us and shed His blood so that we might be saved from sin and born again into eternal life. Now, what I had been learning and engaging with were these sacraments of Communion as the blood and body of Jesus Christ, or Yeshua. The very DNA of Jesus Christ himself. For some years now, I had been taking communion in this way. I was now using it to specifically target the corrupt and disease filled cells within my DNA, within my body. As I took communion, I believed these corrupted cells would be replaced with the incorruptible, perfect DNA of Yeshua. As I began to further explore this healing and wholeness journey, DNA became a huge part of what I was seeing. As I began to engage with this truth, I began to understand the power that His DNA contains.

Mike Parsons states in his blog Freedomarc.blog, 'there is a difference between eternal and living forever. The only reason that I would die is if there is a record of sin within my DNA. I do not need to die, and neither do you. But we do need to undergo transformation by applying the body and blood of Jesus. [...] The Body and blood of Jesus carry the record of the DNA of God. We can age and die, or we can take the body and blood of Jesus within ourselves and live forever.'

John 6:52-58 Crowd: *What is He talking about?* How is He able to give us His flesh to eat?

Jesus: I tell you the truth; unless you eat the flesh of the Son of Man and drink His blood, you will not know life. If you eat My flesh and drink My blood, then you will have eternal life, and I will raise you up at the end of time. My flesh and blood provide true nourishment. If you eat My flesh and drink My blood, you will abide in Me, and I will abide in you. The Father of life who sent Me has given life to Me; and as you eat My flesh, I will give life to you. This is bread that came down from heaven; I am not like the manna that your fathers ate and then died! If you eat this bread, your life will never end.

So, this body, this blood held the essence of Jesus, the very DNA of God within itself; it was the key that held the redemptive, healing power. If I could take on board all that was in His makeup by consuming His flesh and blood, which is essentially His DNA, then potentially, this engagement could wipe out the corrupted DNA in my sick body and replace it with the pure and undefiled DNA of Yeshua, of Jesus. I could engage with the DNA of God.

Now, I had no idea if there was anything happening; I simply continued this daily practice. The months passed as we headed towards June. Business continued to be challenging, having to lay off staff and cut hours. It's not what we had planned for our Pub, this hospitality venture of ours. We had expected and hoped this enterprise would become a huge hub within the community that would provide much-needed employment. It certainly was the former, a hub it had become, but it wasn't thriving from a financial perspective. We were merely making ends meet, which was difficult.

Sometimes living something day in and day out makes it hard to see the end game. Why is it so difficult, why do we have to go through this and what is the result of it all? It's hard to see how anything positive can come out of the everyday trials we face in our lives. As visionaries, as people who want to achieve more and be more, we seek to be overcomers in every area of living. When one area does not measure up, it's hard to see that moment as anything other than a failure. All was to be revealed as the story continued to unfold.

Running parallel to all that was happening with my health and our business, Nancy Coen, the speaker I had been to see in Melbourne the year before, was speaking at a conference in the UK in June and tickets were released around the time I had first received my diagnosis of cancer. There were four inspirational people presenting that week, all sharing some wonderful truths and insightful revelations about the very things that I had been walking through over these past five or ten years. For some reason, this conference was being highlighted to me, and I felt like I would really like to go.

With everything as it was, I put that thought in the impossible file for later on. I mean, our business was demanding, and I could not see how I was ever going to get time off. I was having surgery, and to top it all off, I had never been to the UK or anywhere on that side of the world ever before, at least not in my physical body on an aeroplane. Seriously, I must be dreaming.

Finally, the week before my original surgery was scheduled, the one that needed to be rescheduled had come around, and I was looking for a distraction. I jumped online and thought I would search for further information about the Conference in the UK. It was SOLD OUT. They had a waiting list, so I added my name to the register and didn't think of it again.

A few weeks later, they sent me a notification that a place had become available, and I had 24hrs to claim my spot. I booked it. It was only a conference ticket, no airfares, no accommodation, no other plans. It was an impossible situation; I just didn't think about it again.

We chugged through April, May and there before me on the near horizon was June. My pre-op appointment was on the 4th, and the Conference in the United Kingdom started on the 5th. I had butterflies in my stomach, the ones that are flying so hard they make you sick. There was a feeling in my body that something had been happening, something beyond the normal, but it was just a feeling, it was a belief, and today I would know. I was so nervous because this meant so much more to me than being healed; it was a new way, it was a new path, and if everything happened as I believed it could, then this was the New Now. I'd been a test pilot in my very own experiment; the truth was about to be revealed. I'd had the UK conversation with my husband, and it kind of went like this, "I feel like I really want to go, but it's going to take a miracle" he reassured me it was ok. I packed a small bag and my passport, and I set off on the five-and-a-half-hour drive to my appointment.

The entire journey, I sang and cried. I had the new Bethel Music album playing. The song 'The Goodness of God' was on repeat. Having come through two of the toughest years of our lives, I was now headed to Sydney for a cancer pre-op. To be honest, I felt like there was not too much goodness going on. It was just the hardest song to sing, but I knew I needed to sing it. I kept driving; I kept pressing on. Holy Spirit has a way of helping us push through by throwing us into the deep end when it comes to being undone. It was His nudging I felt to play that song; I couldn't do a thing about it. It was so hard and so liberating that I was completely undone. I told Him, 'My good, good God,' that if I walked into the hospital and the surgeon informed me that there was no cancer, then I would drive to the airport, get on a plane and fly to the UK.

On arrival, I drove around and around trying to find a park, it was Sydney, so it was to be expected. My appointment, on the other hand, was filled with mystery. I was super nervous. Was this the impossible becoming my possible? As I waited in the waiting room because that's what waiting rooms are for waiting, the journey of the past year began rolling through my head. All those things that did and did not happen. Every little piece of this great big puzzle brought me to this 'Now' moment. I could not have imagined that so much was riding on the outcome of today.

"Mrs Henderson", that is me, yes, I'm Mrs Henderson. It was my turn, and I was escorted into a little white room. The Surgeon asked what I was there for, not because he didn't know, but I guess to check that I did. I said I was there so he could tell me I don't have cancer anymore. He looked at me with a serious, doctorly expression on his face. He simply replied, "this is a diagnosed cancer, and cancer doesn't just disappear."

He opened the page on his computer and was looking at the photos of my face. He went on to explain how the surgery was going to be performed and some further details on where it was situated under my eye and the process or finer points of removal before he declared, "We'd better take a look then". He proceeded to closely inspect the area in question, poking and prodding before finally requesting that I make my way into a second white room where he was able to look at my face a little closer. I sat in a large chair, similar to one you would find at an optometrist. Once more, he began to examine the area of my face where the cancer was to be removed. Finally, after a few minutes, he pushed the machine aside and said, "I can't do your surgery because you don't have cancer". I nearly died. Oh my goodness! Inside myself was a rush of emotion, a wave of immense relief and boundless excitement, all flooding through my system simultaneously. I didn't have cancer anymore, and now I was going to the UK.

As I finalised my account, the doctor mentioned to the receptionist that there was a problem, and my surgery needed to be cancelled as I didn't have cancer anymore. They looked a little surprised, to say the least, even perplexed, and I thought it worth a mention that I didn't see this as a problem, that the doctor's conclusion had made my day.

As everything was finalised and I walked from the hospital rooms, I called my beautiful husband, Sean. It was an intense and emotional conversation filled with tears of relief, filled too with the revelation of those words spoken, of those things believed, of all the hard things we had walked through and how every one of them had brought us to this very moment in time. Everything, the hard times in business, the delays and the challenges, they had brought us to this moment, Our New Now! We were living it. We were living just a little on the other side of impossible, our feet were wet, and the huge expanse of water that lay before us felt not so vast after all. I said to God, on the way down, if the cancer is gone, then I'll go, "I'm going to the conference, babe. I'm going to the UK". We were both overwhelmed with the evident confirmation and the craziness that transpires when you begin to believe that anything is possible. Mark 9:23 "Jesus said to him [...] If you are able to believe, all things are possible to the believer."

I drove to the airport. Parked in long-term parking as I did not know how long I would be. Grabbed my bag and passport and jumped on a bus making my way to the international terminal. No ticket, aside from the one I had for the conference. No flights booked. No accommodation; in fact, I had no travel plans at all. What was I thinking? As I arrived, there were two flights boarding, both leaving for London; they were completely booked. The lady at the desk said I might get a flight later but that they would be expensive as it's so last minute. She informed me I'd be needing at least two and a half thousand dollars. Not today. So, I made my way to the flight bookings desk and explained my situation. I needed a ticket to London flying today, and I needed it to cost less than one thousand five hundred dollars. She smiled politely and said there was a heavy demand today that flights leaving now were all fully booked. Just like the lady I had spoken to earlier, she added, I'd be looking at a minimum of two thousand five hundred dollars. She did, however, say she would check the options anyway. She typed and browsed, typed and browsed before pointing at the screen, slightly surprised if not a little amused and explained there was a flight leaving that evening to London. It was just one thousand three hundred dollars; I replied, "That's my flight".

With the flights taken care of, I made my way through customs and proceeded to source a great deal on a rental car and some accommodation for the duration of the conference before boarding my plane; I was on my way to the UK.

Revelation – I am Clothed in Divine Health and Immortality

Activation – Each Morning, as you get dressed, just like you put on your clothes, put on Divine Health and Immortality. As you rub moisturiser onto your face and over your body, declare, 'I am clothed in divine health and immortality.'

Communion–There are many ways you can take Communion; I have used pieces from a few different people's revelations on the subject, many of which are very detailed. Still, in its very simplistic form, this is what I say and believe as I eat the bread or biscuit or cheesecake or whatever you would like to use, and drink the wine, or the water or the juice or the cup of tea. It's not important what you are using, whether it be water or wine or biscuits or bread; only the declaration you are making as you partake in these symbols is important; the fact that by faith, you believe this to be the body and blood of Jesus that is filled with the transforming power of his DNA, the incorruptible DNA of Jesus Christ.

"By Faith, I believe this is your body (Bread) Jesus, the carrier and container of all your pure incorruptible DNA, and this your Blood (Drink) is the source of freedom and life.

"As I eat and drink this, I believe my earthly DNA will transform and transfigure, forgoing the corrupted and mutated pieces from humanity's past and replacing them with your pure and incorruptible heavenly DNA. Thank you, Jesus, that I am in You, and You are in me.

"I am clothed in Divine Health and Immortality."

It is His life, His Light, His blood and His DNA abiding in me, cleansing me and releasing an energy that brings me into the truth of who I really am. It brings me into His divine health and immortality,

11 The Beginning or the End

It was four days ago when we received the call; a friend of ours had been admitted to palliative care given only a few weeks to live. We had planned to visit later in the week; even with all the restrictions, they were allowing four people in to see him at a time. What would we say? How do we navigate conversations about such a final moment in someone's life? The end, it was weighing heavily on our hearts. We have such wonderful hopes to see people healed whole and set free, yet so many continue to die all around us. We had been to so many funerals over the past few years, mortality just became an ever-present reality once again.

Now we sit here just four days later in disbelief as the message comes through. At just 46, he had passed away from kidney failure and with so much life to live, he was gone forever, and we, with our busy lives, were too late. We never made it to the hospital that week. A sadness that quickly grew into anger at our hesitation to visit arose within our bodies, a strange and isolating feeling of no going back, no more chances, and no more we could do about it. That feeling can be so overwhelming that it renders one grief-stricken, sitting in that muddy pit of 'If only.' It's that wanting for closure that you can no longer have. It feels like an empty hole with a constant dialogue from your mind filling the void with thoughts and conversations that can only transpire within the realms of eternity.

What am I to take from this, this piece of time lost forever in the abyss of unanswered questions and the mystery of the end? Every moment has within it feelings that nudge us here and push us there. The wind of His breath that carries within it the way. So many triggers and signs and doorways, yet we still must choose and act, mobilise our destinies and step intentionally into the everyday. Must we be so stoic? Or do we simply become the very change that we want to see in our life, in the lives of others and in our world? Right now, I feel like doing nothing and everything all at the same time.

I have had the honour and privilege of speaking at many funerals over the years. But for all the eulogies I have given, the ones I did not give spoke the loudest to me. It's those I said no to that gave a platform for others to speak; it's those that I said no to that empowered the loved ones left behind that their memories full of hard times and brokenness are legitimate too. So we are giving permission amongst the grief that it's ok to have sadness and anger and confusion and to feel a sense of relief when your loved one or not so loved one passes away. To not see them suffering in sickness or to not suffer beside them as they waste away. To not have to bear the brunt of their frustration in losing mobility or in the clash of personality that was once so easy to avoid but is now blatantly rubbed in your face as you visit and revisit the pain over and over again.

This beautiful, vine-filled winding pathway making its way from the beginning to the end and back to the beginning again is a day-by-day journey of taking hold of joy, love and freedom. It's letting go of comparison, letting go of doing things the way you think everyone thinks they should be done. It's understanding that we are God's plan for change. In becoming a lover of ourselves, we become empowered to love others. It's letting go of shame, that toxic substance that just cannot survive whilst in the presence of the beauty of who you really are. Who are we? We are sons of the Creator of the Universe, a universe that is cosmically inclusive, one that trades shame for bliss, one that says I am fearfully and wonderfully made. A universe that says I am not a mistake, my life experiences do not define me, one that gives us the oil of joy instead of mourning. So step into the forever, step into the authentic you, step into the bliss.

Revelation – People come in and out of my thoughts because now is a wonderful time to reach out.

Activation – Have you been meaning to contact someone, an old school friend, your brother, the old lady across the street, NOW is your moment.

Has someone been on your mind? Reach out, make contact, yes, today. Pick up the phone, send a letter (yes, old school but super powerful) or pop in for a visit. Yesterday is gone… and tomorrow is yet to come. Seize this your moment, your new now.

12 Becoming

As I sat on my flight somewhere above the northern hemisphere on my way to the UK, I began to write in my journal. I was overwhelmed. Never having travelled to this part of our wonderful world before, at least not like this in the physical realm on an aeroplane, I thought to myself, this just should not be happening. This whole scenario within the context of our current situation should have been classified as downright impossible. The knowing within me that I loved and served an incredible and omnipresent God was ever so tangible; I was positively buzzing with possibility. With Him, the impossible is more than possible; beyond our wildest imagination are the things that He can do and more. He was YHVH, Yahweh, He was good, and yes, He was love.

It was there within the distant skies far above countries that until now I had only ever dreamt of seeing that I began to hear the still soft voice of the Father whispering to me. "Becoming." He had instilled in me the revelation that this was not simply a testimony of healing; rather, this was who we are becoming as

His sons and daughters. His word for us was 'Becoming'. The week ahead would be a powerful week for our entire family. This news, No Cancer! This trip, those left behind to fill the gap while I was gone and the testimony of God's goodness that was left in the wake as these events unfolded. I was still being reminded that we are 'Becoming' who we are intended to be. The stories of people I met and places I saw, of rocks, oceans and the heart of a nation of Superheroes, Garden Suites and the restoration of all things. They, in their entirety, were too many to recount. This great adventure to the UK, every place I went and person I met all of them pointed to Him.

One of the things that did happen whilst I was there, although a little silly, was a rabbit trail I followed and happened upon a reminder of sorts. One that we would all be best to remember as we embark on our own unique journeys of becoming as we walk our own paths and roads.

I had brought a Wonder Woman jacket with me that I had picked up for a song at a local thrift shop back in Australia. I had worn it just a few times but hadn't yet washed it. I know you're thinking, "ewww", but it was so shiny and new. Anyway, while I sat in the room with all these incredible people at the conference, I put my hand into the pocket of my gold-winged jacket and pulled out a piece of paper. It was a cinema ticket from two years ago to see Wonder Woman in 3D. I know, Crazy, right. The movie was on the aeroplane on my way home, and I played it on repeat. As I watched, I felt like I had received all that Wonder Woman has as my own, and I realised that what she had the most was that SHE KNEW WHO SHE WAS. She led out of that place of knowing, not to lead itself but rather her knowing who she was, released others into their destinies. I was so inspired, and I felt like the future truly is for the courageous.

The New Now

Courage originates from the Latin Cor, which means heart. (denoting the heart as the seat of feelings) It takes heart to press through fear to be who you were created and destined to be.

So it begs the question, who are you becoming?

As I was writing this book, I took a small diversion for a month or so and began writing a Stand-Up Comedy routine. Now I had never had any kind of aspirations to be a stand-up comedian. Still, I do enjoy writing, and I used to be quite funny in my younger years before I got all serious with the responsibilities of family and life. So, there I was with a partly finished book and a complete Stand-Up Comedy routine. Now, recently I have been attempting to do many things that I have never done before, including fully embracing all that I have ever wanted to be and not just thinking about how wonderful it would be to do all these things but to jump in and begin to step it out, to live it. I contacted some local Comedy guys who were organising an Outback Comedy Tour with some professional Comedians from Melbourne. They were touring small country towns, and they said I was welcome to come along and be a part of the show. The day arrived for my debut performance, and I was petrified. I started thinking, "What am I doing? Why am I doing this?? Am I mad? Have I completely lost my mind? I do not even want to be a stand-up comedian!" I was trying my best to talk myself out of it, with a dialogue of fear, 'what if they don't laugh, because you do know you are not funny', and so on and so forth.

You see, the thing is, I needed to do this. I was breaking through fear. Fear was not having a say in my life anymore. I desperately needed to not worry about what others thought of me. I needed to get up there and do this thing. Laughs or no laughs, this was happening.

To my relief, people laughed quite a lot. The following two evenings, I did two more shows, both nerve-wracking, all completely different, with different crowds, venues and reception, but equally as liberating. There was a strange letting go that began to happen in this process. I was letting go of who I thought people wanted me to be, and I began to embrace the person that I truly was. The part of this process that was most victorious was the part where I was truly becoming myself; I was stepping into the more, into the mystery, into the unknown, the unpredictable. People would say to me, "I could never do that," oh, but you could. You could do something that terrifies you. You could do something that you thought you'd never do. You could do something that breaks those barriers and opens a place where you begin moving forward into your New Now. Yes, it is yours! No fear, your New Now is here and is begging to be taken. Your New Now desperately wants you to step deep inside and explore what you are becoming.

Revelation – When I allow myself to know and feel the Father's love, there is no room in my life for fear.

Activation – Do something you never thought you could. Something that makes you feel alive and pushes the barriers of fear in your psyche. Something that breaks off the preconceived ideas that you have about yourself, false ideas placed there by your own fears and the false declarations of others. Rest upon the revelation that you are loved by the Father of all creation who has a NEW NOW for you. You are Becoming.

"I want to be so consumed by your love that fear's voice can no longer be heard."

13 Finding Your Bliss

Bliss! I just love that word, bliss. It encapsulates the very essence of itself in the wonder of those five sweet letters, five letters just tanked with love. It would not be a complete self-help activation focused book without leaving you with some keys to help you discover this incredible Bliss for yourself. A launchpad to propel you into your New Now, into your bliss-filled future.

It may help if I begin by defining Bliss for you or my version of it anyway. You see, I think of Bliss as a place of encounter. It's the place where I go from knowing that I am in Him and He is in me to the place where I am overwhelmed by that knowledge, and it becomes my reality. It's the place where I press into Him who created me, and I awaken to His divine and unending love for me. Bliss is His Wine, the wine of His love; it is a drunken, messy, deliciously wonder-filled place of connection.

This place of connection can be and potentially is different for everyone; after all, we are unique; some of us like pavlova and others like pumpkin pie, some like watermelon and others ice cream. An entry point to this incredible revelation of His love for us can be one of these things that we enjoy, yes, like cheesecake or going for a hike or swim. I can go for a walk in the rainforest and see moss, I love moss, and it's there that I find myself in the midst of an encounter with His Bliss. I can take a bite of a deliciously decadent chocolate brownie and encounter His Bliss. It's that place where I become overwhelmed by his love for me.

Whatever it might be for you, just be immersed in it, allow the goodness of this connection point to roll over you and then get tanked on the Joy of His love. You can just relax and trip out, or you can be doing something like shopping, you can be at work or in school. It takes all types and all places, and we need the people that fall apart as well as the ones that can keep it relatively together. Just remember I have been legless on the Bliss and if I had been shopping or driving a car, well let's just say that may have turned out a little irresponsible. 2 Corinthians 5:13 TPT "If we are out of our minds in a blissful, divine ecstasy, it is for God, but if we are in our right minds, it is for your benefit. For it is Christ's love that fuels our passion and holds us tightly."

Now the very crazy big reason I know that Bliss is so important is that it is THE VERY ESSENCE of joy itself. Joy, I might add, is referred to in the Bible as my strength. Not just any joy, but the joy of the Lord is my strength. I need joy to be strong; I need this unexplainable place of freedom and goodness, of joy and love to be my foundation. It's the place where I encounter Jesus; it's the middle of His love for me. It's the understanding I have that He is love, that I am in Him, and that I am loved.

Psalm 84:11 (Moffatt), For God the eternal is a sun and shield, favour and honour He bestows; He never denies Bliss to the upright.

Now you might think that sounds like it's only for the well behaved, the noble or the good; well, we are upright because He made us upright, and he has given us Bliss as a free gift. So if we look at Isaiah 59:8, basically, the Lord is saying that all His paths end in Bliss.

The Dominican Monk, Meister Eckhart, spoke of the trinity (Father, Son and Spirit) in this beautiful passage ... "the Father laughs at the Son and the Son at the Father, and the laughing brings forth pleasure, and the pleasure brings forth joy, and the joy brings forth love."

Our beautiful God is truly a God of pleasure, and even though it is our obedience that brings forth this pleasure, it is within His pleasure still that He longs for us to dwell.

Isaiah 48:18 (Moffatt) If you only would listen to my orders, you would have Bliss brimming like a river.

> **Revelation** – God is a God of pleasure, and He longs for me to experience His Wine Barrel Bliss.
>
> **Activation** – Choose something you love. If it's cheesecake, for example, as you slowly eat it, imagine you are surrounded by joy, warmth and love. Picture yourself being loved and being hugged. As you do this, say, 'I am in Him, and He is in me. I am in Him, and He is in me.' I usually end up smiling, feeling His arms around me and feeling a little blissed out, a little drunk, yes, even on chocolate brownies and cheesecake.

You might want to sit in a stream, hike in a rainforest, look at a sunset or close your eyes and picture a green field filled with butterflies and ponies. The point is to connect our place of pleasure with His pleasurable thoughts about us. In this place of connection, we understand we are in Him, and He is in us, and then we begin to encounter the joy of the BLISS.

14 Lightworkers.

Everything that is unfolding before us comes out of union and oneness as we become more familiar with the realms of possibility held within the unseen. As Jesus died and the four-inch-thick veil in the temple was torn, the one that formed a barrier between man and the Glory of God, at that moment, unrestricted access to the realms of heaven and light opened up to all humanity. It is now possible to live the ascended, transcended life right here right now, all the time engaging with the light that is already in us, for He is the light, and within us, He dwells.

As we learn to navigate the unknown pathways and constantly become more aware of everything around us, there are so many circumstances that can trigger us into a heightened emotional state. In this place, we need to turn in and ask, 'Father, what are you showing me?' It's so exciting as our awareness of the pull on the light within me and the light within Him within that collective oneness can bring change. We are the lightworkers, the shining ones; as we come into this place of being, we are no longer trying to do something, but rather we are something;

we are light, for He is light, and joy is our natural position.

We begin to be postured with and live out of the overflow of His goodness as we 'taste and see that the Lord is good.'

'Drink deeply of the pleasures of this God. Experience for yourself the joyous mercies he gives to all who turn to hide themselves in Him.' Psalm 34:8 TPT.

So, take a little sip of the prayer of simplicity, and live within the sweetness of oneness with Him. His light, His DNA, His unending overflowing love within given for the cleansing of us His temple. It makes so much sense in its simplicity and its power. I find it so mind-blowing and so blissfully crazy all at the same time. I love this verse from the Song of Solomon 1:2 'Let Him smother me with kisses- His spirit kiss divine. So kind are your caresses, I drink them in like the sweetest wine.' He is so close to us, smothering us with those sweet, sweet kisses we can quite simply sip of His goodness all day long.

Our currency is intuitive wisdom and love. It comes from oneness, and from this place of oneness, we as lightworkers can rise, enabling us together to shield the world with the manifestation of our united light and love. It all comes from oneness, oneness with Him Yahweh the Divine and oneness with one another.

Light is the energetic life force of love. When we are praying, healing light is released; the more we engage in the heavenly dance of union with Him, the greater the light within us becomes. Jesus says in John 8:12, "I am light to the world, and those who embrace me will experience life-giving light, and they will never walk in darkness." The early church leaders described the Trinity using the term perichoresis (peri – circle, choresis – dance). The Trinity was an eternal dance of the Father, Son and Spirit sharing mutual love, honour, happiness, joy and oneness.

It's the light that runs through us that causes us to operate at a higher frequency; we can engage with the truth of who we really are; we are sons of light, sons of love. Turn into the light in me, the Christ in me, for He is the light of the world. As mentioned previously, we are called to the things Jesus did and greater things than these. Imagine doing greater things than Jesus. God, our Father, has predestined these things for us, for just like Jesus, we too are his sons.

We can engage with light technology, His Light DNA. Just as when we take communion, those little pieces of Him become one with us, releasing their transformative power. 'Taste and see that He is good, he has come, and we are clean. He has given us another whole level of living, tapping into the light technologies of union with the Divine nature of God, true life and immortality.'

We have so much to be joyful about; we are in union with the divine nature of God. We are held within the fiery furnace of His everlasting love. He is igniting the light within us to burn so brightly, bringing protection in this bubble of light and love. All of this is inwards if we turn inwards, remember the simplicity of You loving Him and Him loving you. It's called the prayer of simplicity. Brother Lawrence, a lay monk who served as a cook in the monastery of the severe order of Discalced Carmelites in Paris, France, during the 1600s, discovered the secret to cultivating holiness by "practising the presence of God" in the ordinary business of life. He is quoted as saying, "I have abandoned all particular forms of devotion, all prayer techniques. My only prayer practice is attention. I carry on a habitual, silent, and secret conversation with God that fills me with overwhelming joy." "There's no greater lifestyle and no greater happiness than that of having a continual conversation with God."

Final Words

My beautiful friends, we have but dipped our feet in the ocean with the words written on the pages of this book. I have wanted ever so much to introduce you to the beginnings of this revelation, to invite you into the spaces and realms of light where you can lay in the green pastures with Yeshua, with Jesus. You can begin to plant and explore your own garden with Him, the garden within your heart. This has been a multi-decade journey for me; the exciting part is I absolutely believe that your journey of discovery will be accelerated; you will reach heights and discover mysteries in timeframes unheard of twenty years ago.

The first seventeen years of marriage to my beautiful husband, we were on very different pages when it came to the things of the spirit. But after those years had passed, he had his very own revelation of God's Love. During a wild road trip, whilst riding a three-wheeled motor-tricycle around the outside of Australia with myself and our two boys, Sam and Josh, Sean had a very real encounter with Jesus in the middle of the

Northern Territory, on the road inside his motorbike helmet in the heart of the Outback, no churches, no preaching, no altar calls, no people. Just him and Jesus. Following this encounter, he decided to go to Bible College and served as an intern with a pastor there for ten months. The Holy Spirit spoke to me about this time at college, saying, "I am going to do in Sean in ten months what I did in you in ten years." WOW, that is a lot, and it was. It was a miraculous transformation in every aspect and on every level of his life. There was an incredible expansion of his capacity to receive and process revelation. His understanding and wisdom grew exponentially, and his walk was quickened in a way that led him to relate to others who had lived and walked in this way as sons of God for many years. It was just like he, too, had travelled the road many times before. If anything, his journey greatly challenged long-time Christians as he walked with such wisdom, such authenticity, such passion and love.

This, my beautiful friends, is the space where something supernatural is set into motion, where we can be seated in rest and still find ourselves immersed in the limitless places of acceleration. Accelerated revelation, accelerated absorption and truth. We are stepping into a time of discovering and understanding wisdom that has been stored up for such a time as this and knowing wisdom herself. It is time to understand that we are all just beginning, and we are all in this 'New Now' together. Together in oneness.

We live in the times when we can receive a download of information right onto the hard drive of our mind, where we can be given an increased capacity to process this information and turn it into new technologies, new solutions, and higher ways of functioning. It is a time of wild spiritual encounters;

many will look like unsolvable problems from the outside but become divine hope and wonderous solutions in the spirit.

As many longtime believers often call people who have only just come into the revelation of who Jesus is 'baby Christians' or 'new Christians.' I am here to tell you that there will be a limitless release of Godly wisdom to these young ones, to these beautiful new creation sons, yes! We declare a limitless flow of His goodness, not just double or triple or even one hundred-fold, for we are moving into the limitlessness of the age of the kingdom, the age of perfection in Him. They are not to be relegated to junior positions of faith for these hungry ones, these bold and courageous ones, these ones who have just realised there is a light within them and have switched it on. They will run like the wind, they will not grow weary, they will walk and not faint, and they will love with a love so ferocious that it begins to set the world on fire. People will look, and they will say, these are those we have been waiting for, these are the sons, they know Him, they know The Way, The Truth and the life of Yeshua. These are the ones who will bring forth restoration; these are the children of light.

What He did for us, so unfathomable, so inconceivable, has meant we are able to live an everlasting life of divine health and immortality. By this light that shines from these passionate ones, we can see the impossible become possible in our lives, and we are able to step into the fullness of a life of freedom and hope lived in the light. A life drenched in His wonderful and unquenchable thirst for us, a life saturated and resonating with His eternal Love. In many ways, we are all amateurs, beginners on this journey of discovering the new now; I have included below a list of those whose relationships and teachings have encouraged and helped me discover this new way of living.

The resources, books and podcasts that these amazing people have put together are well worth listening to. I am always led by the Holy Spirit when I am engaging in and learning new things. With the Holy Spirit and wisdom as your guide, everything flows together and begins to make more sense, even when you are learning something from here and another thing from there. If you are just starting out on this crazy road of discovery, there is lots to take in, so just buckle up and enjoy the ride.

If you are looking for more, here are some of my favourites:

Further Reading and Podcasts.

Justin and Rachel Abraham – Company of Burning Hearts

Bill Johnson – Bethel Church

Mike Parsons – Freedomarc.com

Peta Condon – Heavens Reflections

Ian Clayton – Son of Thunder International

Nancy Coen – Global Ascension Network

Footnotes and References.

Beep Beep – Lyrics by Godfrey Birtell

The Passion Translation – Dr Brian Simmons

Mike Parsons – Freedomarc.com

About the Author:
KYLIE HENDERSON

Kylie is a creator, artist, songwriter, author and lover of the great outdoors. She and her beautiful husband Sean have two amazing sons, Sam and Josh and together have nurtured a passion in life for all things adventure. This passion for more has taken Kylie on a crazy spiritual journey, one of which she shares within the pages of this insightful and inspiring book. She is a passionate lover of God on a quest to tap into the fullness of what a relationship with the Creator of all creation looks like. We are all amateurs as we walk these unknown pathways into the future. It's so exciting to have you on board.

Shawline Publishing Group Pty Ltd
www.shawlinepublishing.com.au

www.ingramcontent.com/pod-product-compliance
Lightning Source LLC
Chambersburg PA
CBHW011317080526
44588CB00020B/2739